COME WHAT MAY, COLBY GREY

By: Johnny A. Sanders

LaVa Publications
Webb, Alabama

DEDICATION

Melinda has been my partner, supporter and "life" for forty-two years and she is the mother of our children, Chris and Melanie.

After retirement, Melinda encouraged me to create stories for our grandchildren, Blake, Parker and Shayna as I had done for our children. From that encouragement and her belief in my abilities as a storyteller, she inspired me to write my first novel.

I, therefore, dedicate this book to my loving wife, Melinda W. Sanders.

A special thanks goes to Linda Russell, Martha Becker, and Amy Vrasic.

BIOGRAPHY

Johnny A. Sanders was born and reared in Phenix City, Alabama on October 21, 1937. Johnny was welcomed by an average family who had relocated to the mill town from rural south Alabama farms during the 1930's.

Johnny's father was a policeman and detective in Phenix City. His mother was very caring and hard working. She often worked double shifts in cotton mills, leaving Johnny in the care of his older brother. Johnny's imagination grew during these summer days which was carried over into high school and college dramas and creative writing classes.

Following a successful high school and college football career, Johnny became a football coach, teacher, principal and finally retired as a guidance counselor.

FORWARD

Come What May, Colby Grey is a twist of events of love, sex, hatred, revenge, murder and drugs dealing with the wealthiest family in Atlanta, Georgia. Colby Grey, one of the most expensive private investigators in the United States and located in Atlanta, becomes the employee of this family.

Jennifer Myland, one of the most beautiful women Colby had ever seen, hired him to find her husband, Jason. Jason had supposedly committed suicide several months before, but Jennifer was convinced that Jason's death was a hoax.

Jennifer's sincerity and charm convinced Colby to accept this case. The extreme twist of events leading to the solution brings out the very best in Colby Grey in Come What May, Colby Grey.

COME WHAT MAY

PART 1

CHAPTER ONE

Thursday, December 8, 1988

Just this afternoon a very beautiful young widow by the name of Jennifer hired me. She did not believe her husband was dead and wanted me to find him or produce evidence that his death had been a hoax. Every private investigator has a curiosity level and mine had been ignited. Perhaps it was her beauty or maybe it was the eyes that I had looked into that made me want to find out why she thought it was a hoax. She told me how her husband's remains were returned from a hunting trip where he had allegedly taken his own life. The gory details made my stomach weak as I heard her explain what had happened.

Jason, her husband, had been an avid wild boar hunter and would take several days annually to hunt in the mountain country of Georgia. He built a cabin high in those mountains that served his needs for these yearly trips. He never took anyone with him on these excursions because it was a time for him to get away and be totally free from the city world, she explained. However, he went up each month to check on the cabin. On October 21, 1988, Jason left for his yearly hunting trip and she never saw him again. On October 28, she was notified that Jason had shot himself with a 308 high-powered rifle. Next a lightning storm about the same time had struck the lodge burning all the contents of the cabin along with Jason's body. The only way to identify the body was through his dental records.

1

Jason's insurance company was satisfied with the police investigation as well as their own examination and had submitted the payment of a million dollars to the beneficiary, Jennifer Myland. However, she was not sold on the idea of his death, particularly not suicide. She felt that she knew Jason very well, and he would never take his own life. There was nothing in this world that would have caused him to take such drastic measures. He loved life too much; and he never would have had the courage needed to end his life.

She had convinced me, Colby Grey, the most expensive private investigator in the South, that her husband's death might be a hoax. I told Mrs. Myland my fee was $1000 per day plus expenses. Also, I explained there was a fee of $25,000 should I solve the case. But, if I had not found something within one week our agreement would be terminated. She agreed, and I became the employee of Jennifer Myland, one of the wealthiest women in the United States.

Most investigators have certain habits they do that help them think better, mine is walking at night. Walking at this time makes me more relaxed and gives me a chance to reason out details of a case and helps me to find the starting point, the motive, or maybe just the beginning of a case. It helps me understand certain events or important facts of a case. Sometimes it makes me wonder why I take a case in the first place. That is exactly where I am now, wondering why.

This case may be a hopeless cause, but I am sure it will be a pleasure working for Mrs. Myland. My concern is will she be able to accept what the investigation unfolds. If indeed her husband's death was a hoax, what could the reason be? That is what I am being paid to find out and to give a reason one way or another. The investigation may bring some things out about her husband that will make it hard for her to accept. My findings could tear his life apart, his personal life, and his business life and yes, even his intimate life with his wife. Could she accept it if Jason had committed suicide? At any rate the investigation will begin in the morning, come what may.

CHAPTER TWO
Friday, December 9, 1988

This morning is like every other morning with one
exception, that it is the first day of a new investigation.
There will be five more days in which I must come up with
something that will give probable cause for the death of
Jason Myland. I found myself hoping there would be some
evidence to support her belief because I like the idea of
working for one of the most beautiful women in Atlanta. In
fact, probably the most beautiful woman I had come in
contact within my ten years as a private investigator. Yes, I
would say the most beautiful.

I usually arrive at the office around 8 A.M. making notes
and planning my day as to what, where and how the
investigation would be conducted. My secretary, Jean
Young, a 43-year old mother of five, was already at work
when I arrived. She knew my habits well and was not
surprised when I arrived at work almost an hour earlier than
usual. New cases seem to get my thought processes in
motion.

Jean Young was not only my secretary but also a very close
and dear friend. Someone I listened to when she has
something to say because she is always honest, sincere and
straight to the point. After giving her the details of the case,
her only comment was "Colby, these people are very
powerful – please be careful."

Leaving the office, I went straight to City Hall to read the
sheriff's report on the death of Jason Myland. Little did I
know this would take me until 10 A.M., as it was the

longest report I had ever seen. It covered Jason's death with a fine toothed comb. There was nothing in the report that pointed to any kind of foul play. His dentist, Dr. James Owens, clearly identified the teeth of the remains found in the cabin as those of Jason Myland. Jason's pipe lighter, which bore his name and date of marriage, was found in the cabin. His 308-rifle barrel was also found next to the body along with his belt buckle.

I couldn't put my finger on it, but I felt that something was missing or left out of the initial report. Maybe I was hoping for something to reach out and grab me, saying there is a reason for Mrs. Myland's doubt of her husband's suicide, as it was reported. However, there was nothing in the sheriff's report that made me think otherwise. Evidence is what I must have in order to continue working for this beauty, Jennifer Myland. The *Atlanta Ledger* Newspaper office was my next stop. I wanted to see if any leaks had materialized from that end. Many names were mentioned but none that caught my eye. Pictures of the graveside service showed hundreds of people attending. He must have had a great number of friends. I had the paper run me a copy of the coverage, so I might peruse it later in more detail. You never know what can be missed the first time, and it always pays to look, cover, and study many times as you search for clues.

My next stop was Jason's office in the Building of Glass. The company Jason worked for was the largest computer company in the South, owned and operated by his father-in-law, Gilbert Skinner. I called Mrs. Myland and asked her to meet me at the office. Maybe I would have a little more freedom to do what I wanted to do while searching his office with her present. Family members sometimes make a difference when you are trying to do an investigation and do it correctly, particularly if it's the daughter of the owner and president of the company!

Jennifer Myland met me at 11:30 A.M. in front of the Building of Glass. She suggested that we have lunch before we went to Jason's office and I agreed. We went to Rami's Restaurant, a nice quiet place with just the right atmosphere, and the food is superior. Lunch was delicious made even more so by a beautiful and delightful lady. We talked about little things that were important to her; how Jason looked forward to his hunting trip each year, and how he was a creature of habit. He always went the same day, the same month, the same time of day, and most of all took the same clothes and the same food each year. He always returned on the same day, no matter how good or how poor the hunting happened to be. He always had a small party with a few close friends and family members after returning from his hunting trip. This was important to him; it enabled him to come back to the realities of his real world.

As we finished lunch, I insisted I pay the check because I was on an expense account. She agreed with the most beautiful smile I had ever seen. Problems could occur for me from this case because of Jennifer's (she informed me earlier that she would prefer being called Jennifer not Mrs. Myland) ability to touch my inner self. I welcomed those kinds of problems: beauty, wealth, and success.

When we reached Jason's office, Ginny Sharpe, Jason's secretary, didn't want to let me in. After Jennifer explained I was her private investigator, I was allowed to enter without any further discussion. The office was as large as my entire apartment. It consisted of a kitchen, a large bath, bar, and a sitting room. As I looked through his desk, not knowing what I was looking for, I was hoping something would capture my attention. I found his own personal smoking tobacco, one I had never seen before, because it was a special order from the factory. Strawberry Rainbow Smoking Tobacco is a distinctive name for a particular brand of tobacco. The smell was tranquilizing, one I had never experienced, and one I surely would never forget. There was nothing but a great deal of files and reports about the business in his office. I noticed some personal pictures of his hunting trips and a few names and appointments he had set up prior to his death. He had loved his hunting for sure because his pictures were dated back to 1980, his first wild boar kill. He was definitely a creature of habit because every picture was posed the same way with every minute detail identical. However, something bothered me about the pictures; I couldn't put my finger on it, yet.

After going over the office carefully, I came up with nothing that proved to be any help. This bothered me because it was now 3 P.M. and the first day was passing fast. My next stop would be the dentist office. I called, explaining who I was, for whom I was working, and what I wanted. It was no problem getting an appointment to see Dr. Owens. It was set for 4:15 P.M. Saying good-bye to Jennifer, I was off and running to see Dr. Owens and was hoping for a clue to spring forward just any time now.

Dr. Owens was a very pleasant man who had been Jennifer's dentist long before becoming Jason's. He was very cooperative, showing me Jason's entire file, the same file I had seen in the sheriff's office earlier this morning. There was nothing really out of the ordinary with Jason's teeth. He kept his teeth in good condition according to his records; and Dr. Owens said, "Jason's teeth were remarkably clean for a heavy pipe smoker." After speaking with the nurse, I learned that Jason liked to flirt with the women. According to her, I could learn more by coming back next week and speaking with the hygienist. She was not working this week because her family had been involved in an accident in Texas. Her name was Martha Rogers, and she supposedly knew Jason better than anyone in the office. I will make it a point to speak with her when she returns to work on Monday.

Leaving the dentist office, I went back to my own office to see if I had any messages. I did. The most important one was from Jennifer. She wanted me to return her call at home. As her phone rang, I wondered if she had found or remembered something important concerning the case. When she answered the phone she sounded out of breath; so I asked if anything was wrong. She replied that she had been in the shower and didn't know how long the phone had been ringing. Visions of Jennifer in the shower made me break out in a cold sweat. Her physical features had to be perfect in every way; I guessed 36-24-36, a perfect figure to go along with a most beautiful face. Her reason for calling was to invite me to come to dinner and discuss the day's findings. I gladly accepted, if for no other reason just to get better acquainted with her.

As I drove to Jennifer's, I thought how wonderful it would be to make love to a woman like her. She had everything a man could want or need - looks, figure, personality, intelligence, and wealth. Why would a man commit suicide with a wife like Jennifer waiting at home for him to come back to? It just didn't make sense. There had to be a reason for Jason's death other than suicide, but what? I had not come up with anything that would prove my hunch as of the first day.

To my surprise, Jennifer, filled with beauty and class, answered the door. She had on a low cut dinner dress that exposed two lovely mounds and it fit every curve of her body to a tee. Her long black hair was down over her tan shoulders and her dark eyes sparkled. She was truly unbelievable.

After dinner, we sat and talked about what the first day of the investigation had brought. There was nothing I could tell her with the exception of the possibility that Jason may have been a flirt with the women. She was not surprised how someone might take Jason's friendliness for flirtation, but there was no other woman in his life, she decided.

Later, crawling between the sheets, I thought about how strongly Jennifer had felt about her husband. Why and for what reason did he commit suicide? Maybe Jennifer's idea of his death being a hoax is true. Now all I have to do is find the proof.

CHAPTER THREE
Saturday, December 10, 1988

I was not on pay roll or expense account on Saturdays, but I decided to work anyway. There was plenty for me to do, but first I had to go to the office and pick up my notes. Usually Jean Young would have my notes typed, but today, I would have to make out my own scribbling, since she was off on weekends.

When I arrived at the office, to my surprise, Jean was behind her desk typing my notes. She had coffee already made and she had found some addresses of the places I needed to go this morning. I told her to call John Lindsey and tell him to be free next week. John is my legman; he does the majority of checking people out and running down leads for me. Jean said she had called John yesterday, and he would be free and here Monday morning. She knew my every move and took care of it before I asked, in most cases. Thank goodness for a secretary like Jean.

Three cups of coffee and two hours later, I told Jean I was going to Atlanta's Smokers Corner and later to Kennesaw Mountain. I also told her to go home and spend some time with her family. Do what she needed to do, and I would take care of everything on this end. I knew today was her big day for cleaning, shopping, and cooking for her family. Yet, here she was at work doing things that I needed done for this case. She is truly amazing.

Finding a parking space on Saturday in downtown Atlanta is not easy, but I guess I'm just lucky. I pulled my red 911 turbo Porsche into a parking space just up the street from Smoker's Corner. I only hoped this was Jason's tobacco shop. If not, maybe they could give me some lead as to which shop it might have been. Since I don't smoke, I didn't know many tobacco shops; but I had seen this one advertised on television and remembered its name. It gave me a starting point.

The young girl in the shop had never heard of Strawberry Rainbow Pipe tobacco. The manager happened to be coming from the back of the store and overheard our conversation. He immediately told me that type of tobacco was ordered from the company. He went on to explain that it was very expensive, costing $10 a pack, and most shops only purchased it when the customer was able to order by the case. Ten dollars a pack is rather expensive for pipe tobacco; however, when you are worth millions you can spend what you want for it. It is evident that Jason had excellent taste in fine smelling tobacco and beautiful women, like his wife and his secretary.

When I asked if he sold this tobacco to any customers, his reply was no; but his uncle's shop on the other side of Atlanta did. In fact, his uncle had ordered some just last month and might still have some. He offered to call his uncle's shop to see if any of the tobacco was still in stock, thereby saving me a trip across town. He returned after a few minutes with the bad news that they were out of that tobacco, but would be happy to place an order on Monday. After finding out the address, I told him thanks and left. Maybe there's something here, but I had to hurry because the shop closed at 1 P.M. and it was after 12 P.M. now.

As I arrived, the gentleman's uncle was locking the doors; but was kind enough to open up and take my order. The least he would order was a case, which was five cartons or

25 packs, and that added up to $250 plus $20 for shipping. He told me my tobacco would be in Friday of the next week.

It was lunchtime; and since I had only had coffee this morning, I was hungry. Ed's Restaurant was on the way back to the office, so I stopped and had lunch. When I finished it was almost 2 P.M. Time flies when you are having fun or working on a case you like, and I like this case or should I say, I like my employer.

The rest of the day and night were spent at the office going over small things in my notes, things John could start on Monday when he begins his probing into some of the lives of the people surrounding this case.

CHAPTER FOUR

Sunday, December 11, 1988

Today is my day for rest, one that is spent doing what I want and like to do. I am a football nut, and I usually go to the Falcons' games; but today I am going to Kennesaw Mountain to see if any evidence was left unturned by the sheriff's department.

After driving to Kennesaw Mountain, I found the area where Jason always left his car. He then continued into the mountains by using a 4-wheeler because the terrain was rough, and it would take two or more hours by a regular car. Unfortunately, the 4-wheeler wasn't available, and I didn't want to spend two hours trying to reach the cabin so I decided that I would return on my own 4-wheeler on Monday.

During my drive back to the city, my thoughts drifted toward Jennifer. Forget it, Colby, she's your employer, and you never have mixed social life with business associates. However, there had never been an employer like Jennifer before. Even though I know she is out of reach, I can still think and fantasize about her.

Back at my apartment, I had a call on my answering machine from Jennifer. Why would she be calling today? Returning the call, I wondered if she was in the shower again, or if she would be out of breath when she answered? "Hello" a beautiful voice answered. She wanted to know if I had found anything at all that might support her theory that Jason's death by suicide was a set up by someone. I couldn't tell her yes because there was nothing concrete. Yet my ole gut feeling said she was right. She sounded disappointed then surprised me when she said, "What do you have planned for tonight?" Because I hesitated, she quickly added, "Colby, if you have plans it's okay, don't worry. I just needed company tonight and didn't want to be alone." My answer this time was quick and to the point, "I have no plans and would certainly love your company tonight or any other night." Now that really did sound forward.

I made reservations at the Elite Dining Room for 8 P.M. which would be perfect. The Elite Dining Room had a lounge and dancing area. After dinner we danced a couple of times and she didn't disappoint me at all. She was a soft stepper and as light as a feather. As I held her in my arms and glided across the floor, I thought, "What a fool Jason was if he did indeed commit suicide."

When I took Jennifer home she invited me in for a nightcap. I accepted. She told me how much she appreciated my being with her tonight. Also, she asked me if I needed anything for the next week. I thought that was a strange question and couldn't figure it out. Then the bomb hit me; she was to be gone all next week, and probably would not return until Friday night or Saturday morning. She told me if I needed anything to call Ginny Sharpe, and she would take care of it for me. I hated to say good night but I did and left.

CHAPTER FIVE
Monday, December 12, 1988

Today begins the second true day of the investigation, and I must find some evidence to support my gut feelings. These impressions are highly influenced by my attraction to Jennifer, and it is of great concern to me. No one has ever gotten next to me the way she has in such a short period of time. Maybe her being gone this week will help me get back to my normal thought patterns. Therefore, time is very important, and I need to pace myself to use every minute to the advantage of the case.

Jean had coffee made and had stopped to pick up donuts. She is a woman that knows my every want and knows that I love donuts in the morning with coffee. I had eaten three donuts with two cups of coffee before John Lindsey arrived.

After filling John in on the details of the case and how far I had gone, we decided what each would do today. I was going to the Kennesaw Mountain area, while he would check out the rest of the tobacco shops and a list of people we believed were involved in the case. I was very careful not to let John know my own impressions; I wanted him to be open-minded in his investigation.

According to the police report, there was a country store at the entrance of the woods where Jason always picked up supplies. As I spoke with the store owner, Kayo Carter, I found everything Jennifer had told me about Jason being a creature of habit to be true. He always bought the same items for his trip. His shopping list consisted of a half a dozen cans of sardines, half a dozen cans of Vienna sausages, half a dozen cans of tomatoes, a box of saltine crackers, and two loaves of bread. The list also contained two items he dearly loved; bologna and a case of Royal Crown colas. Other necessities included a small jar of mayonnaise, a dozen eggs, a pound of bacon, half a dozen cans of vegetable soup, two bags of ice, a fifth of Jack Daniels's and a couple of rolls of toilet tissue. The owner also told me he was dressed the same way from his hat to his boots every time he came hunting.

As we talked, I realized this man knew everything that went on in this area. Of course, that is true in a small community such as this. If you want to know what is happening, go to a store and you can learn about everything and everybody of importance in that community. So as we talked, I found out that this man knew Jason well. He also told me that Jason broke his routine only once in all the years he had been coming to Kennesaw Mountain. That was six years ago when he brought his wife with him. He explained she was quite a looker, small, very neat, high class, very attractive and had beautiful long hair. That was Jennifer all right, beautiful, high class and very attractive.

Kayo was very sure about the items Jason purchased. He was meticulous in his record keeping; the type and quantity of each item was logged in his credit book. Jason always sent him a check for $100 a week after his trip. That was more than enough to pay for his supplies with the exception of when his wife had come with him. He bought her a $400 gold lapel watch pin. He also purchased a specialty item of snake skin boots that had steel climbing spikes on the side of the boots and steel toes. The spikes were for climbing trees, Jason related to Kayo. However, there was no mention of spikes or steel toes in the report, and I wondered if this could be the first clue that would help me with my gut feelings. Kayo had been very helpful, and I thanked him as I left his store on my way to the scene of the shooting.

As I followed the map that I had taken from the newspaper, I couldn't help but wonder why a man would go to such trouble to hunt animals. This terrain is very rocky. I had left my 4-wheeler 30 minutes ago and had a rough time traveling the path to the cabin. This trip just proved to me that I am a city man at heart and will surely stick to hunting people, not animals.

After viewing the burned out site, I realized Jason knew what he was doing when he built his cabin. It was protected on two sides by the walls of the mountain and the open view to the front, which made it difficult for anyone to get to the cabin unexpectedly.

The sheriff's department must have done a super job investigating this case because there was nothing at the scene to help me. I had gone over the cabin very thoroughly and there was absolutely no evidence or clues that were overlooked by the county investigators. I could not believe there was not one piece of evidence somewhere to give a reason why this happened; or did Jason just flip out and truly take his own life? Could there have been that much pressure on him and if so, from where? Was it his job, his home or his personal life? I must find some concrete evidence and soon.

Everything in my section of Atlanta had closed down for the day when I got back to the office. There were messages on the phone, and also Jean had left me a page of notes from her day of work. None of them were important enough to return at this hour of the night so I compiled what I had learned today and filed it in my desk drawer. As I was about to leave, a knock came from the door. I felt to see if I had taken off Sara (my .357 magnum named after my first love Sara Mandell), luckily I had not, so I went to the door and opened it.

John Lindsey greeted me with a big smile and a loud "hello". He came in, got himself a beer out of the refrigerator, and filled me in on what he had found during his investigating. There were purchases of Rainbow tobacco from all three of the tobacco shops. Each shop had one customer who ordered a case monthly. However, the purchaser never picked up the tobacco. The wife always came in, paid for, and picked up the shipment. Each shop had about the same ordering date, which was the last week of the month and the same delivery date during the first week of the month. At one stop, the person placing the order was Henry Lott, at another shop the man's name was Brian Rollins and at the third shop it was Steve Howard. The only description the shopkeepers could give about the wives of these tobacco smokers was "pleasant and attractive". John had also spent some of the day at the dentist's office speaking with Martha Rogers. Martha's aunt had been killed in an automobile accident last week in Texas and her mother had taken the accident and death very hard. Consequently, Martha had spent the entire week in Texas. John had earned his salary for this day because he had already been in touch with Texas and confirmed the accident, the name of the deceased (confirming it was Martha's aunt) and that Martha had in fact spent the week in Texas.

I told John I wanted pictures of Ginny Sharpe and Martha Rogers as early as possible Tuesday morning. Also, I remembered a picture of Jennifer on Jason's desk, but I would have to figure some way to sneak it out past Ginny Sharpe. Not only was her last name Sharpe but she was sharp as well.

As I drove home, I couldn't help but think about Jennifer. Where was she, what kind of trip had she gone on and who was she with tonight? The answers to these questions were easy and simple; it is none of my business. I am an employee of Jennifer Myland and nothing more.

Chapter Six
Tuesday, December 13, 1988

This begins the third day of the investigation, and I have very little evidence to go on. There is nothing that would indicate Jason's death is anything other than suicide. Usually by the third day I have enough evidence to support my theory, but not this time. My only hope is that today will bring me closer to the truth of the shooting.

It was getting late in the morning, and my first stop was the Building of Glass. Ginny Sharpe, Jason's secretary, didn't want me to go in his office again; but Jennifer had told her to give me what I wanted or needed. I explained how important it was for me to see his office again. Ginny, being the good secretary she is, complied and allowed me to enter the office. I thought how much Ginny and Jennifer Myland were alike. Both had long dark hair, both were tan, and both were built about the same. Even their mannerisms seemed to be similar. Their faces were different in shape, but Ginny was still a very attractive woman. I smiled as I passed her desk, and to my surprise she smiled back.

As I searched the pictures on the wall of Jason's office dealing with the hunting trips, I did not see Jennifer in any of them. Five years ago would have been 1983 but for some reason that was the only year that was missing a photograph. Each picture, beginning with the year 1975, had a big boar at Jason's feet but there was no picture for the year 1983. I am sure that was the year Jennifer went hunting with him. My attention then turned to Jason's desk and Jennifer's picture. I took it out of the frame and put it under my coat. As I left the office, I told Ginny thanks and that I owed her dinner sometime. Her reply was quick, "Just let me know when."

My next stop was at the dentist office to speak with Martha Rogers. Maybe there will be some concrete information to come from this meeting because there are a number of questions I want to ask Martha and hopefully she will have the right answers.

Upon meeting Martha, I could not believe what I was seeing, a woman that could pass for Jennifer's sister. I could certainly see why Jason would be attracted to Martha, if indeed he had been. The resemblance to Jennifer was amazing. Her hair was not quite as long nor was it as dark. Her eyes were real light blue, unlike Jennifer's dark brown eyes. There was a big difference in the two; but they could still pass for sisters, particularly if you didn't know either of them.

Martha was a very pleasant woman and talking with her was easy. According to her, she only saw Jason when he came into the office for his dental appointments. For some reason I didn't buy her answers because her eyes didn't seem to be saying the same thing as she was relating with her mouth. Her eyes seemed to light up every time she mentioned Jason's name. Martha must have read my thoughts because she explained her beliefs to me and how seeing a married man would be totally against her moral values. She had been married once but had been divorced about three months ago. Her husband, Jack Rogers, had left town some three weeks ago and she had not heard from him since that time. She had no idea where he was or what he was doing. His occupation was construction and he moved from job to job and from one part of the United States to another. That was the reason they had come to Atlanta six years ago.

John and I met at Rami's at 3 P.M. to go over what we had discovered during the day. John ordered lamb chops, and I ordered a T-bone steak, medium well. While waiting for our late lunch, we discussed the day. John had gone to the tobacco shop in the Kennesaw Mountain area and discovered that they sold a case of Rainbow tobacco each month to Jason Myland. He always picked it up the first week of the month. This had been going on since 1980 according to the owner of the shop.

We finished our lunch around 4 P.M. John took Jennifer's photograph and was off and running. We were to meet at 6 P.M. back at the office. I paid the check and walked out into the fresh sunshine. It felt awfully good at this time of year. As I looked up and down the street, I could see people, already in the Christmas rush, hurrying in and out of stores. This is my favorite time of the year, and I always look forward to the Christmas season.

John called the office and left a message with Jean Young that he would not be able to make our 6:30 P.M. meeting, but I had said 6 P.M. He would explain later this evening or meet me at 8 A.M. in the morning at the office. This usually meant he had found something and was not letting go of it. Maybe he had found 'that something' we have been looking for since last Friday. I will try to place each piece of the puzzle in its right place, hoping to come up with something to tell Jennifer when she returns this weekend.

There were several messages on my answering machine at the apartment, but the most important one was from

Jennifer. She is finishing up her business trip early and will be back in Atlanta Thursday afternoon. She wants me to make arrangements for a meeting with her that evening. A meeting with her will be no problem at all, not at all!

I had a couple of bourbon and cokes as I watched television. Sometimes reruns are worth watching a second time, and Miami Vice certainly was tonight. As most of the Miami Vice series were dealing with cocaine, tonight was not an exception. Cocaine is easy to get and is worth millions of dollars on the streets in the United States. It is amazing what people will do to obtain drugs.

Just as I was getting ready for bed, the phone rang. It was Ginny Sharpe, and she needed to talk with me tonight and could we meet at the Top of the Night Lounge at 11 P.M.? I told her I would be there before 11 P.M. I hung up the phone, got dressed, put Sara in her cradle, and was ready to leave at 10:22 P.M. It should take me about 30 minutes to get to the Top of the Night Lounge.

At 10:45 P.M., I parked my car and got inside the glass elevator on my way to the lounge at the top of this forty-story building. Some ride. When the doors of the elevator opened, I could see Ginny waiting for me at a table in the corner. I walked across the floor toward her, wondering what could be so important that she had to talk with me tonight. I smiled as I approached the table but did not receive one from Ginny in return. I could tell she was very nervous and afraid of something before I sat down. Her eyes gleamed with fear, which I spotted as soon as I stepped off the elevator.

As I sat down, I asked her what was wrong and why was it so urgent for us to speak tonight? She began by telling me that she was a very good, loyal and hard working secretary. I told her that I knew she was and that I respected her for her loyalty, but what does that have to do with tonight? She asked me to please listen and let her explain, which I did from that moment on. She was typing orders and letters from Jason's dictaphone today when she ran across a message from Jason. It was a personal message to her, and she doesn't know how to handle it. Jason knew he could trust her because he had trusted her so many times in the past.

Jason had a safe installed in his office and no one knew about the safe except the two of them. There is a list of names in the safe that Jason wanted her to turn over to the police if anything should happen to him according to the message she found. She was afraid after hearing the tape because she realized this might prove Jason had been murdered. She wanted to know what she should do because the safe was well hidden and probably would never be found. If it were found, the finder would not be able to open it. Jason was the only one with the combination until today, and now she knew the combination. I then began to ask her some questions. Did she tell anyone else about the message? Her answer was, "No," she was too frightened to tell anyone. What did she do with the dictaphone that contained the message Jason left? She had put it in her filing cabinet and locked the cabinet. Did she open the safe? "No way" she explained. I asked her one last question, "Did anyone notice that you were nervous or upset before leaving work? "Yes, Mr. Skinner's secretary wanted to know what was wrong." She was a quick thinking young woman because her answer was, "Yes, it happens once a month every month."

There was nothing we could do tonight; we couldn't get into the building this late so I suggested that I take her home and meet early in the morning at her office. She didn't want to be left alone; she was too frightened. Was there someone she knew who could stay with her tonight? The bomb exploded with her next statement. She would feel a lot safer knowing I was with her.

When we got to her apartment, I told her I would sleep on the sofa. She let the sofa out and while she made the bed, I checked the apartment and everything was in order. Then she took a shower to get ready for bed. When she finished her shower, I was already tucked in for the night. We said good night to each other and turned off the lights. As I lay there I thought how lovely Ginny was and what a beautiful personality she had to go along with her loveliness. I fell asleep thinking of Ginny.

I awoke about 2 A.M. to go to the bathroom, and when I returned Ginny was in the sofa bed. I looked down at her, she looked up at me, smiled and said we are two consenting adults. As we made love slow and easy, I saw how beautiful her body was and how good it felt next to mine. After we finished making love, I realized just how lovely she really was. With these thoughts, I fell asleep with her in my arms.

Chapter SEVEN
Wednesday, December 14, 1988

At 8:30 A.M., Ginny and I were walking into the Building of Glass. I could not imagine what Jason meant by a list of names. I would soon find out as we were now entering Jason's office. Ginny went into the restroom and called for me to come inside if I wanted to see the safe. I thought I had gone over every inch of the office, and I had not seen anywhere that a safe could be hidden. Just then, Ginny opened the shower door and pulled open a hidden panel. There it was behind the faucets. Ginny turned the hot water to fast and the cold water to slow which was the first part of the combination. The second part of the combination was three numbers 19, 8, and 13. She turned right to 19, left to 8, and right again to 13. The final part of the combination was to turn the hot and cold water back to off. Ginny opened the safe and began to remove items. Among the items were over $200,000 in cash, three long envelopes, and a .38 Colt revolver. Where did Jason get so much money and why did he have it in his personal safe? The first envelope contained a list of stores in Atlanta. The second one contained a bill of sale to an apartment in the Atlanta Plaza. The third envelope had a list all right, but it was not a list of names, but a list of numbers. The numbers ranged from 01-26.

Ginny was just as puzzled as I because there was no list of names and because of the amount of cash in the safe. I asked Ginny to hold off calling the police and let me try to solve Jason's code. She put the money back into the safe and I kept the three envelopes, which I deposited into my coat pocket. She closed the safe then the hidden panel, and came out of the shower. She told me she would delay telling the police for two days. Hopefully, that will be enough time to crack his code. I asked Ginny to type me a list of names of people Jason did business with and people he knew who were not business associates. She promised me the list when I picked her up for dinner tonight (the one I owed her from yesterday). I said that sounded like a great idea, and I could hardly wait until tonight. Ginny laughed and I left headed for my office.

Jean had told John I would be late coming in because of my stop this morning. John wanted to know what I had found out about the case. After I told him of the night before (leaving out certain details), I filled him in on the morning events. He also told me his findings and why he had not met me last night.

He had discovered that each store pointed out Martha Rogers as the wife of their buyer who ordered the case of tobacco each month. John had followed Martha after she had gotten off work yesterday. However, it was a fruitless evening. She went to her apartment and didn't leave until this morning when she returned to work. John had stayed with it all night so it was home and bed for him while I would try to make something out of this list of numbers.

I got another cup of coffee and went to work on the numbers. My first impression was that each number was a letter of the alphabet, but when I put the numbers down and matched them with the letters, it spelled absolutely nothing. There had to be a key to these numbers, and I had to find it before Friday. It seems that everything I tried was out of the ballpark and I had not gotten any closer to solving it at 5 P.M., when Jean came in to tell me she was leaving for the day. I knew I had to leave also because it was getting closer to my dinner engagement.

When Ginny opened the door, my heart skipped a beat. She was so gorgeous dressed in a white dress. Her tan body and dark hair went so well with the white dress. Last night she was attractive; but oh my stars, tonight she is not only beautiful but so radiant looking. As she walked to her bedroom to get her wrap, I watched her lovely body move side to side, and I thought maybe we should skip dinner tonight. But since I had not eaten anything except a BLT for lunch, I decided we better go have an excellent dinner. You never know when you may need it later.

As we ate dinner and drank wine, we talked about our day. She told me Mr. Skinner came by and wanted to know if she had found anything important in Jason's office. Her answer was no, but was told if she found anything of importance to inform him immediately. Also Mr. Skinner's secretary came in three times during the day to offer her assistance with Jason's dictaphone tapes. That was awfully strange, she related, because Mr. Skinner's secretary never offered to help anyone. At least that had been her policy until today. Even with all this going on, she had found the time to type me the list of names that I had requested this morning.

After we had finished dinner, Ginny wanted to stop at her movie rental store to get a couple of movies. This was fine with me because I enjoyed watching a good movie once in a while. After picking out <u>Fatal Attraction</u> and <u>3 Men and a Baby</u> we stopped at the beverage store to pick up a bottle of White Star for later tonight. Now we were all set for a quiet evening at home.

As we watched <u>3 Men and a Baby</u> we talked about the list of numbers we had found in Jason's safe. After listening to the way I had tried to solve the code, Ginny made the statement that Jason always liked to do things backwards. For example, when looking at a magazine he started at the back and flipped to the front page. If I start at the back of the alphabet with Z being zero one, it may give me the right system to break the code. This might be the break I need.

We put <u>Fatal Attraction</u> in the VCR and opened the White Star. Ginny had already slipped into something more comfortable to enjoy the movie. This was a good movie, and we both enjoyed it. I couldn't help but think what an awful feeling it must be to make one mistake, and it takes over your whole life. Ginny had enjoyed it more than I had because she had really gotten into the acting part. I always try to figure everything out and every move before it happens. This was one of the best movies I had seen in a long time.

Ginny came over and sat on my lap and said, "She told me I had better watch out for you." I asked who SHE was and she replied, "My Boss." She looked at me and put her left hand on my face. Then she brought her right hand up and cupped my face. With this she moved her face close to mine until our lips touched and we kissed a long, passionate kiss. She was some kind of lady. After several long kisses, we moved to the bedroom. As we undressed each other, I thought what a wonderful way to spend time working on a case.

If I thought last night was wonderful, I was wrong because it would have to take a back seat to tonight. Ginny is an incredible lover. As we made love, she told me things all males like to hear. "You're good, you have the right touch, and you're wonderful" and the ultimate was when she said that "I was the best man she had ever had". I told her how "good she was" and how "wonderful the last two nights had been for me". As we lay in the bed where we had just made passionate love, we talked about Jason's habits, and finally, I realized that in order to get my work done, I had to leave this delightful creature who was lying beside me.

Ginny wanted me to stay the night with her, but I had to get back to the apartment to work on the list of numbers. I told her good night, how wonderful she was again, took the list of names she had typed, and left. That is what I call dedication to a case, especially when you leave something as beautiful as Ginny to go to work.

Upon returning to my apartment, I began working on the code Jason had set up with the numbers. I took the first name on the list and tried to match letters with the numbers but the code was difficult to crack. Starting at the back of the alphabet with Z being the number zero one and working toward A as number twenty six was not the code although it did produce certain letters that looked as if they were in the right place. For example, the first set of numbers on the list had four numbers in the first name and three numbers in the last name. The numbers were 23, 12, 21 and 13. The last name numbers were 09, 14, and 02. When I matched them with letters it looked like this: DOFN and RMY. Unfortunately not one name on Ginny's list had a combination of four and three letters in their two names.

At 3 A.M., I stopped working because the letters and numbers were all running together. I took a shower, made some fresh coffee and tried to think how I would set up a code like this. After drinking two cups of coffee, my eyes cleared and I was ready to get back to the code.

I decided I would check the number of letters in the names on my list with the same numbers on the number list. There was a name that had seven letters in the first and last name. The numbers were 20, 22, 25, 15, 18, 09, and 07 in the first name while the numbers in the last name were 08, 24, 22, 13, 13, 18 and 09. The name that will match the numbers with seven numbers in each was Gilbert Skinner. Number 20 would be G and it worked but how would the rest of the numbers fit with the letters. That's it! Fit the numbers with the letters, not the letters with the numbers. If these fourteen numbers will make Gilbert Skinner's name or give enough letters with numbers, to match, I may be able to break the code.

At 6 A.M., I finally broke the code. Z was zero one and numbered backward in the alphabet to N, which was number thirteen. Beginning with A as number fourteen, then counting forward to M which was number twenty six gave me the code. When I broke the code, I began to write down names from his list of numbers. The first name on Jason's list of numbers (the combination of four and three) spelled out the name John Ray. Who is John Ray and what part does he play in this case?

CHAPTER EIGHT
Thursday, December 15, 1988

There were ten names on Jason's list of numbers. I recognized some of the names but most of them I had never heard before. Gilbert Skinner and Jack and Martha Rogers were people I knew but the rest of the list was new to me. The names that were unfamiliar included John Ray, David Shaw, Joyce Dexter, Quinton Coppin, Rodney Day, Kwee-Un Ji and Tracy Love. These names are very important to the case, and hopefully John will be able to trace down the person who is attached to each name. He has certain contacts in different departments of the government who can locate names and people. That's one reason why John is so important to this investigation; his connections are willing to help him.

Driving to the office, I tried to place Jack and Martha Rogers in the case. What part could they have played? Did their divorce have anything to do with the case? Could they be a part of the death of Jason?

John was waiting at the office, smiling when he met me at the door, wanting to know about the list. Did I break the code and if I had, were any of them people we knew? As I read the list to him, he was as surprised as I was about Gilbert Skinner's name being on Jason's list. I also told him about Skinner wanting Ginny to let him know if anything of importance turned up about Jason. Then there is Skinner's secretary. All of a sudden, she wants to be helpful by offering her assistance to Ginny. According to Ginny, this was quite a shock because she had never offered her help to anyone before. Why would she offer her help now? Being a good Samaritan was not her usual behavior.

John made a copy of the names and began calling his connections. He was told it would take several days to locate these people and to find the area where they are living. Of course, there is always the possibility that they won't be able to locate them at all. However, if anything turns up, they promised to contact John immediately.

We had a number of things that had to be completed before noon. John was going to see Martha Rogers and also wanted to find out what he could about her husband, Jack. He had a tracer put on Jack earlier this week. He also wanted to check out Jason's apartment at the Plaza, his home away from home or was it just an investment?

I needed an appointment with Gilbert Skinner, so Jean called the Building of Glass and made an appointment with Gilbert for 10:30 A.M. I thought about the importance of this appointment and what method of approach I must use. Jean's words kept coming back to me. "Be careful Colby," she pleaded, "these people are very powerful people." I believed her and also understood this would be a very interesting appointment.

The president's office was on the top floor, and it made Jason's office look like a cabin at the lake. It was a beautiful layout with everything Jason had plus much more. This office had a bedroom and a huge bath area with a hot tub, and there was a room that was closed off from the rest of the office. I wondered what could be in that room. Just then the door opened, and Gilbert Skinner entered the room. He was a large framed man, very neat in his appearance and attire, and gave the impression of importance.

Mr. Skinner was about 60 years of age with gray hair. Jennifer must have gotten her beauty from her mother because her father was a rough looking man with none of Jennifer's features. He was a very intelligent man and well-educated. He spoke as if he were a graduate of some Ivy League University. I knew the questions I asked him would have to be thought out very carefully. If I was not watchful, he may have me answering his questions instead of him answering mine.

Mr. Skinner and I chatted for over an hour before he ordered lunch for both of us. It was one of the most stimulating conversations I had been involved in for a long while. I had to be on my toes every second of the conversation. I liked the way he answered questions with questions of his own. Sharp! He was a very astute individual. I could understand why he was so successful in the business world.

He believed that Jason had committed suicide. He had spoken with Jason a few days prior to his hunting trip and thought him to be awfully depressed. However, he did nothing to indicate he might be considering suicide. Jason had been having some personal problems as well as some business problems. His main responsibility in the business was security. He was in charge of all security for the company, and he had let an individual enter the security force with a questionable background. The man's name was Jack Rogers.

Keeping up with Gilbert was a job because he gave you what he wanted you to know and nothing more. He could read a great deal into a statement. He surprised me when he slipped questions in about Jennifer. How long have you known my daughter, and what kind of relationship do you have with her? I know he could sense the anxiety in my voice, but he accepted my answer for the time being anyway. He is keenly aware of Jennifer's beauty and the power of persuasion she has on people because he made the statement that she could wrap anyone around her little finger. I felt as if he was firing that remark at me.

After spending two plus hours with Gilbert and having a 12 ounce T-bone steak, I was ready to talk with someone who would enjoy small talk. Therefore, my next stop would be Jason's office to see Ginny. As I entered the outer office, I did not see anyone. Ginny was not at her desk nor was she in Jason's office. It was 12:30 P.M. with about 10 minutes left in her lunch break, so I decided to wait for her. About 12:57 P.M. the secretary from the outer office came in from lunch. I asked her what time Ginny would be returning. Her reply was, "Ginny did not come in this morning, and it is strange because she didn't call in sick." I reached for the phone and dialed Ginny's apartment. There was no answer, so I left the office in a run, headed for Ginny's apartment.

As I arrived at Ginny's apartment, there was nothing unusual going on so I took a deep breath and tried to relax. The door was locked. I rang the doorbell and knocked several times, but there was no answer. I took a credit card and opened the door. The apartment was just like it was when I left last night. Ginny was not here, and there was no evidence of physical violence or any kind of struggle. Where was she and why hadn't she called in this morning? Was I worried about Ginny? Yes, very much!

Leaving Ginny's apartment, I went back to my office, arriving about 2:30 P.M. to find John and Jean both gone. This puzzled me. Why was Jean gone, and where was she at 2:30 in the afternoon? I looked around to see if she had left me a clue as to her whereabouts. I saw the note on my phone. It said that Mrs. Myland had called and wanted me to meet her at the airport at 4 P.M., Flight #1896 from New York, gate B-15. It also said she was trying to find me to give me the message; if she didn't she would meet Mrs. Myland at 4 P.M. Jean is some kind of lady, and the best secretary a guy could have in any kind of business.

The time was ticking by because it was almost 3 P.M., and it would take me at least 45 minutes to get to the airport in the downtown traffic. Just as I was leaving, the phone rang; it was Jean checking to see if I had returned to the office. I had been waiting to find out if that was Ginny calling. It wasn't, so I hurried out of the office to my car hoping I could get to the airport before Jennifer's flight arrived.

Thank goodness her flight was 15 minutes late because I had just gotten there when her plane landed. As she exited the plane and headed toward me, I saw her beautiful smile, and I knew it was for me. I couldn't imagine how a man could want another woman with her at his side. Her charm seemed to radiate ahead of her as she drew closer. My mind began to wonder, where had she been and what kind of business had she been taking care of in New York? Then all of a sudden she said, "Hello, Colby, how have things been going for you?" "Fine," was my reply and before I could say anything else, she wanted to know if I had been able to prove that Jason's death was not a suicide. I was sorry to disappoint her with my answer, but she kept smiling coming at me anyway.

It was 5 P.M. by the time we picked up her luggage and managed to get into the traffic. We talked as we drove back toward Atlanta. I told her of the week's investigation; but when I mentioned the safe in Jason's office, she was shocked. She was not aware of any safe in his office and certainly never knew he kept that kind of cash on hand. She wanted to go to his office before they closed the Building of Glass. It would be closed at 6 P.M.; so we had to hurry. The 5 P.M. traffic was horrible.

I asked Jennifer if Jason had taken photographs of every year he had been hunting. She confirmed this and further stated that he always killed at least one boar each year, and the boar always lay at his feet when the photograph was taken. "You saw all those photographs in his office last time," she reminded me. My next question puzzled her. I asked if Jason had not gone hunting in 1983. She said, "Yes, wait a minute, one year I believe he had to fly to London, on an emergency for the company and couldn't go. That might have been in 1983. Why? Is that important, Colby?" "Could be, I don't know just yet, but it could be", I replied.

We got to the office with time to spare. Jennifer went straight to the safe and began screaming. When I got to the bathroom I saw Ginny lying on the shower floor, naked and with her throat cut. There was blood everywhere; she must have put up some kind of fight or either she was tortured before she died. Her clothes were scattered all around her as they had been ripped from her body.

I felt as if someone had poured acid on my insides. Ginny was very important to me, and now she was gone. There was an empty feeling in me right now; one I had not experienced in a long time. We had gotten close to something, Ginny and I. I did not know exactly what it was at the moment but you can bet I will find out what it is and I promise I will find the person or persons responsible for her murder.

I poured Jennifer a brandy and called the police. While waiting for them to arrive, I looked in the bathroom and shower area but saw no clues that might lead to Ginny's murderer. I was very careful not to touch anything. The $200,000 was gone, and there was only an empty safe and Ginny's tortured body. After about 15 minutes, the police came in giving orders, telling us not to touch anything and to stay where we were until the lieutenant arrived. He would probably have a number of questions to ask us. I felt I had failed Ginny in some way and I couldn't blame anyone for this except myself because I had missed something that was very important to this case.

CHAPTER NINE
Friday, December 16, 1988

Whoever killed Ginny was going to pay if it was the last thing I ever did. She had been someone very special to me and she was murdered because of the contents in that safe. Someone was worried about me solving the puzzle. The safe contained important pieces to that puzzle, and sooner or later I will find where they fit.

I had been up all night at the police department, hoping they might have come up with something about Ginny's death that would be helpful. A professional had killed Ginny – it was obvious.

As I headed for my apartment, I remembered I had to meet John at the office at 10 A.M. Oh, well, at least I will have time to shower and change my clothes, I thought. When you are a working man being paid a thousand dollars a day, you can't worry about a little thing like sleep.

When I arrived, I discovered that my apartment had been torn apart, clothes everywhere, chairs, sofa, and the mattress had been cut up. Even the freezer had been emptied on the floor, but they had not found what they were looking for. The office would be their next stop. Oh my God, Jean would be there in a matter of minutes because it was 7:30 A.M. and she was always there before 8 A.M. I had one hope; maybe she stopped at Joe's Donut Shop to pick up some donuts. Looking for a number in the Atlanta telephone directory can take hours when you are in a hurry. Finally, I located it. "Joe, this is Colby Grey. Is my secretary, Jean, there, or has she been there this morning? My heart skipped two beats when he said, "Mrs. Young,

Mr. Grey would like to speak with you." I told her to stay in the shop until I got there, not to go anywhere near the office, and that I was on my way to the donut shop.

My office was my next stop. With Sara in my hand, I checked the elevator and it was on the floor of my office. I pushed the button for its return to the first floor. When the door opened, I placed a chair in the elevator so the doors couldn't close. It couldn't make a return trip to my office floor. The only other way up or out was the stairs. I was already going up the steps three at a time. As I approached the office door, I knew someone was in there, tearing it apart. He had not found my hidden compartment on my desk because he was still looking and never saw me as I entered the room. When I spoke, he turned toward me and at the same time threw a knife. As I dove to the right over a chair, I felt the cold steel of the knife cut into my left arm. All in the same action, he was running toward me with murder in his eyes. The ring of Sara stopped his movement as I shot him in the leg. He gave no indication of pain because, as he hit the floor, a .38 special appeared in his hand. The second ring of Sara stopped all movement as it tore part of his chest out. It stopped the scream of the intruder.

Jean had seen me enter the building and called the police. They came shortly after the shooting. Jean had come in and was helping me when the paramedics arrived. Lt. Black, who is a personal friend of mine, came in about the same time. He wanted to know what happened. After telling him what I could but leaving out certain details, he went about the office trying to piece things together.

By the time Lt. Black had finished questioning me, John walked in wanting to know what had happened. I told him everything that had happened since I saw him last. He did not know about Ginny until the morning paper had arrived. He had been on a stake-out at Martha Rogers' apartment until about 3 A.M. before going home.

John had found some good information about Jason's apartment. It had served as a love nest for Jason for years. According to the neighbors, there had been at least three different women who spent time there with Jason. John said Martha and Ginny had been identified with Martha being the last of the three women to spend time there. In fact, she had been there as late as the later part of November.

John had gone over the apartment very thoroughly to see what he could find. Traces of cocaine were found in the bedroom, bathroom, and kitchen. However, we had not found any evidence to point to Jason as the user of the cocaine. The amount of money I found in his safe might prove he was a dealer of cocaine in some way. Why would he be a dealer with the kind of money and life style he had? It just didn't make sense. But, the pieces of the puzzle are beginning to fit and hopefully they will fall into their proper places soon.

John left to speak with Martha Rogers again while I headed for the hospital. I was told I would need some stitches and a tetanus shot as well as antibiotics for infection purposes. Jean wanted to take me but I refused her and went alone. This proved to be a bad decision because the shots the doctor gave me were strong enough to knock out a bull. There were a total of 18 stitches, eight stitches on the inside and 10 on the outside. The wound was deeper than I had imagined. I was very drowsy when the doctor finished, and I knew I couldn't drive back to the office. Then, an angel walked through the door of the emergency room. Jennifer had called the office earlier and had her chauffeur drive her straight here, thinking I might need her help and she was right.

As we drove back to the office, Jennifer wanted to know every detail of what had happened this morning. After I had gone through everything, she asked me to explain why I knew my office would be hit next and that the perpetrator would still be there. I told her the intruder had not found what he was looking for in my apartment and that is how I knew the office was his next target. I knew he had left my apartment just minutes ahead of my arriving because the ice in the ice trays had not completely melted after being dumped on the floor.

Jennifer looked at me and smiled, then said, "You are very thorough with your observations, Colby Grey. I now know why I hired you." She handed me a check for $6,000 for the five days work plus expenses. I had not solved the case yet but had begun to step on someone's toes and it looked as if suicide may be last choice for Jason's death. If Jason is dead, he was murdered.

As we entered the office, Jean had gotten things back to normal with coffee made and the usual fresh donuts served neatly. After having a donut and a good cup of coffee, I asked her if John was going to return after his meeting this morning. She answered, "Yes, he will return around lunch and wants you to be sure and be here, since he has gathered some new information."

Jennifer told me she had to get to her office for an early appointment and she must leave immediately. This woman continued to amaze me; she asked me to have dinner with her tonight. Of course, I accepted; and yes, I would be there at 6 P.M. I thanked her for her help and assured her that I would not forget the 6 P.M. dinner date. She left with a smile on her face. One that would excite anyone; it sure did me.

John was about 30 minutes late getting to the office. He had to wait for his cover man to arrive to relieve him in the surveillance and possible tailing of Martha Rogers in case she went some place during lunch. He had opened his bag of tricks while talking with Martha this morning. He had told her about Ginny's death and why he thought it had happened. Even though Ginny's murder was reported in the paper, it didn't tell anything about her being tortured before the final blow that killed her. I had stayed at the morgue all night to find out if anything out of the ordinary had happened to cause her death. She had been cut in several places that could not be seen because of the blood covering her body. That explains why she opened the safe for the killer. She had been tortured so cruelly that she could not stand the pain. Her killer had cut off both nipples of her breasts and she had cigarette burns in her genital area.

John said he had not gone into full details but did tell Martha some of the cruelty that Ginny had suffered. He noted that Martha Rogers was indeed a cold woman because it didn't seem to bother her one bit that another woman had been tortured so badly. John believed that she was in some way involved in this case and that is why he was now tailing her 24 hours a day until the case was solved.

Jean told me the tobacco shop had called to let me know that my smoking tobacco shipment had arrived. She also said they had overcharged me $8.33, and I could pick up my refund when I came after my tobacco. How could they have made a mistake on the amount they charged me when he took the price of the tobacco and freight charges from one of Jason's invoices? They had charged me the exact price they had charged Jason. Maybe the cost of the tobacco has gone down since I ordered. That is not likely; if anything, the price should have gone up, not down. At any rate, I will find out as soon as I pick it up. Maybe I can go to the shop later this afternoon or the first thing in the morning.

By the time John and I finished our meeting, it was time for me to begin preparation for my dinner engagement with Jennifer at 6 P.M., which was only an hour and a half away. I was really excited about this dinner; it made me feel as if I were a high school senior again. I did every thing I needed to do; shaved, showered, changed clothes, combed my hair and brushed my teeth. I was now ready to drive to Jennifer's for dinner.

CHAPTER TEN
Friday, December 16, 1988

The butler asked if I would like something to drink before dinner as he granted me permission to enter Jennifer's home. My answer was no and he motioned for me to follow. I could hear voices, a male's and female's voice, but I was not able to make out the male's voice until I entered the huge den area, and I realized it belonged to Gilbert Skinner. There he stood and I knew Jennifer had to have gotten her beauty from her mother because there was absolutely nothing that reminded me of her father. That is unless it was her keen sense of business since Gilbert Skinner was one of the most brilliant minds in the business world today according to *Business World Magazine.*

Dinner was all business, not exactly what I hoped for earlier, but then I'm just an employee. Jennifer had wanted me to go over every detail with her and her father. While drinking our after dinner coffee, I told them everything I wanted them to know. I got the feeling Skinner knew a great deal more about Jason's safe than he was letting on, especially the contents. I had gotten the same feeling when I told Jennifer about the safe on the way from the airport the day Ginny was murdered. Things I had not related to them were known, I thought. Neither they nor I ever mentioned the $200,000. They asked questions about Jason's apartment in the plaza and wanted to know if I had checked out the apartment. If so, had I found anything of value? Also they wanted to know if they could see the apartment Monday. Of course, Monday would be fine with me. I would meet them there at 9 A.M.

When I finally left Jennifer's house at 9 P.M. Gilbert was still in our presence; he had camped right there with us the entire night, not that I ever hoped to stay any longer myself, but I can dream, can't I? The dinner had not been what I had expected and I left feeling as if I had been on trial and I had failed very badly according to the look on Gilbert Skinner's face. That man really bothers me for some reason, but I can't place a finger on why. Maybe it is his sense of superiority over people.

As I drove to the office, I called John and told him to meet me there. I also tried to come up with a reason for the feeling I had for Gilbert Skinner. Maybe it was some of the things Ginny had told me about him and the way he treated everyone who worked at the Building of Glass, even his son-in-law. Then, I thought maybe it was the way he watched me when I was around Jennifer, as if he was afraid I was going to touch her or worse, even make a pass at her. Maybe it's because she is spending a lot of time with me on this case. I can't blame him because I would do the exact thing for my daughter, if I had a daughter.

Our list of names had been shortened by two. When I arrived at the office, John was waiting for me. I told him we had two more faces to go with our names. First, Kwee-Un Ji, the intruder I had killed earlier today; and second, Rodney Day was an alias for Lieutenant Ronald Peak, one of Atlanta's finest (on the drug force). We now knew over half the list; with luck we could complete it in a couple of days. My plan was very simple, keep the names that we knew on the list and change the five we did not know to fictitious names. Then, give the list to Gilbert Skinner to make up different names with the same number of letters. Let's see if they can break the code. John was puzzled because he didn't think I was telling anyone about the list. I assured him I had not, but Skinner knew about the list. Maybe Ginny had let it slip when Skinner questioned her. He had brought it up in his twenty questions tonight. Of course, he could have gotten Jason's dictaphone from Ginny. Then he would have found out about the safe and the contents. There is the possibility that Ginny let the cat out of bag. If she did, it might have cost her her life. Only time will tell, but believe me I will find the answers. When I do, it will lead me to the ones responsible for Ginny's death. They will pay, whoever "they may be."

John and I left Gilbert Skinner, Jack and Martha Rogers, Rodney Day, and Kwee-Un Ji on the list. We added Ginny and Jason's names along with Ronald Peak. Kwee-Un Ji also had an alias, Kid Young, which we added and threw in the words Atlanta Plaza to make the list complete, that is, this list now had ten names as did the original list.

That is the list we made for Gilbert Skinner. I know it's not ethical to withhold information from your client, but Jennifer was my employer, not Gilbert Skinner. However, Jennifer had told me to release anything and everything to Skinner. So that is what I must do; that is what I am doing, releasing a list to him.

John had found Jack Rogers' apartment today but was told he had not been seen for several weeks. He had paid for the apartment through the month of December. The landlord would not let John enter the apartment and look around, even though he had been offered a C note. He told John not to return until the end of December.

Arriving at my apartment, I found it clean and in order.

Jean had called my cleaning service earlier. Thanks to her, I was able to relax. I will get a good night's rest; I need sleep badly. Saturday and Sunday will be scheduled for rest; at least it will give my arm some final mending time before the stitches are removed next week.

CHAPTER ELEVEN
Monday, December 19, 1988

After resting on Saturday and Sunday I was able to meet Skinner and Jennifer at the Plaza apartment at 9 A.M. There was nothing there to interest either of them. After 30 minutes, Gilbert said he had a meeting that wouldn't last long with a friend and would I meet him at his office at 11:30 A.M. I told him I would and that I would bring the list of names at that time. I left and went straight to the office to see if anything new had turned up over the weekend.

Lt. Black had called. Upon returning the call, I learned there were two types of blood found on Kwee-Un's knife. One was mine and the other was Ginny's. What I had expected was true, Ji was the one who had tortured and killed Ginny. I just wish I could have made him suffer the same way he had made Ginny suffer. I thanked Lt. Black and hung up.

It was getting close to the time to leave in order to keep my appointment with Skinner. I arrived at his office at 11:25 A.M. He was not there and he kept me waiting until 11:45 A.M. This was to my advantage. His secretary gave me some information about Ginny's private filing cabinet where she had put Jason's dictaphone tapes. They had not been able to open the cabinet until this morning because of the police investigation. Skinner had no way of knowing about the list unless Ginny had told him. (Did she tell him about us?) I reported the discovery of money to Jennifer but not the amount so she must have gotten that information some place else. Where is the $200,000? Kwee-Un Ji didn't have the money with him, and the authorities had not located his vehicle as of this morning.

When Skinner arrived, I gave him the list of names and explained that the code had not been broken yet. I would continue working on it but if he was able to break it before I did to please let me know. I gave him the deed to the apartment at the Atlanta Plaza, which I had failed to give him earlier. I told him I was running late for another appointment and had to leave. But before leaving the building, I stopped by Ginny's office to have a look. It was still taped off by the police, so that was out of the question.

I spoke with the outer secretary about Ginny and the day she was killed. But office secretaries have to remain loyal and quiet and she knew nothing. She was upstairs most of the morning helping Mr. Skinner's secretary, running off material for the yearly board meeting that was scheduled for the end of the month. She had not heard or seen anything out of the ordinary. I asked her if she often helped Mr. Skinner's secretary. Her reply was, "Once in a while when Ginny was running behind with Mr. Skinner's demands." Thus my next question, "Was Ginny running behind with the board meeting materials?" She answered, "Not really, because she still had some typing to do on stock holders pages. We usually wait until everything is typed, then we run it off, put it together, and then we're completely finished." I told her thanks and asked her not to mention our conversation to anyone. She wanted to know if she had done something wrong by telling me what had happened. I advised her that it would be best that no one knew that we had talked. I then left, and as I looked back at her, she had a worried look on her face.

My next stop was at the Tobacco Corner. They apologized profusely about their mistake and refunded my money. The owner was not there and would not be back for a couple of days. I told the employee I wanted to speak with the owner when he returned and left my business card with her. I promptly left.

When I returned to the office, Lt. Black had called to say they had found Kwee-Un Ji's vehicle. It was a rental under an alias name and nothing was found in the car except his fingerprints. Where is the money?, I asked myself. What did he do with it? Find the money and we may be able to solve the case.

I wanted to talk with Martha Rogers again so I called the dental office. I suggested I come by the office or meet her at her apartment, but she wanted to meet at the Varsity, a popular drive-in restaurant near Georgia Tech University at 6 P.M. After my conversation with Martha Rogers, I told Jean to get in touch with John and tell him to bring the pictures of Ginny and Martha by the office in the morning. I was planning another trip to Kennesaw Mountain in hopes of finding out some answers to questions that have been unanswered.

I arrived at the drive-in at 5:45 P.M. and waited for Martha to arrive. At 6:30 P.M., I left as she had not shown up. I went back to the office to pick up the list and see if I had any messages. The first one was from Jennifer thanking me for helping her with her father. Second, there was one from a young lady by the name of Joan Harrison. She said she would call tomorrow. The third was from John telling me that when I received this message he would be on a flight to Houston, trailing Martha Rogers, and would call later. So that's why she didn't meet me; the heat is getting hot and she's running.

CHAPTER TWELVE
MONDAY, DECEMBER 19,1988

I decided to sleep at the office in case John called when he arrived in Houston. The assumption was a good one because John called at 2:45 A.M. He was in the Houston airport calling me, watching Martha as she waited for her luggage. He had disguised himself so she would not know he was following her. She was now reaching for her luggage, and he wanted to be outside before she went out the door. He said he would call later then the phone went dead. I thought I would make some coffee, work the list, and wait for John's calls.

As I reviewed the names we didn't know, John Ray, David Shaw, Joyce Dexter, Quinton Coppin, and Tracy Love, four males and one female name remained. I did not have a clue about these names or the people using them. There is a connection between the names on the list and Jason's and Ginny's murders. I must find that connection. First, I went to the phone directory and began listing names and phone numbers. There were nine John Rays in the phone directory and six with an initial of J. in their name. Jean will have a chance to work on her phone conversation today. After finishing my list, I noticed it was 5:05 A.M. and John still had not called. I decided to lay down on the sofa and relax for a few minutes.

CHAPTER THIRTEEN
Tuesday, December 20, 1988

At 7:03 A.M. the phone rang and woke me from a deep sleep. It was John, telling me he had followed Martha to what appeared to be her family's home. It was a small house with a picket fence surrounding it, nothing out of the ordinary. He had to wait for the corner store to open to use the pay phone because it was inside the building. (As usual the battery on his cell phone did not get properly charged prior and during this impromptu trip.) He could see the house from where he was standing; he had already changed his disguise and was waiting for a rental car company to open so he could have a car delivered. Hopefully, Martha would not leave any time soon. However, he retained the taxi just in case she did decide to leave. I then asked John if there was any way I could get into his apartment to get the photographs of Ginny and Martha. John's answer was sweet music to my ears. He had put them in a locker at the airport and left the key in an envelope with my name on it. I could pick it up this morning at the airport locker. "Thanks John, maybe we are closer to finding the answers we need for this case. Talk with you later, be careful out there in Texas," I told him. About the time I hung up, Jean came in with donuts and wanted to know if I had slept here last night. "Of course, what little I slept," I replied with a smile. Then I told her I was about to leave for the airport and then to Kennesaw Mountain. Also, I told her about John, where he was and not to expect him today. "Oh, yes! I almost forgot," I added as I grabbed a donut on the way out "If Joan Harrison calls find out what she wants but let her know I'm not taking another client at this time; as I am involved in another case."

CHAPTER FOURTEEN
Tuesday, December 20, 1988

After leaving the airport, I began my drive to Kennesaw Mountain. Personally, the way I felt about Gilbert Skinner was not good. He has to be involved with the case. I only hope Jennifer's not involved in any way. I wondered if Skinner could be the mastermind behind all this calamity. I am convinced that both Jason's and Ginny's deaths were planned. The $200,000, where is it? Is it dirty money? Evidence is sure pointing in that direction. What part does Jack Rogers play in this case? Where is he today? Why did Martha Rogers run to Houston, Texas, when I wanted to talk with her? All these questions have to be answered soon. That is if we are to solve this case within the time limit.

Upon arriving at the country store, I wanted something hot because the temperature was dropping fast. I got a cup of coffee and asked Kayo, the owner of the store, to join me. He did; and as we talked, I asked him had he been able to remember anything else about Jason that might help me. His answer almost knocked me to my knees. He told me about Indian Joe. "Joe lives at the high end of the mountain. He doesn't see many people and not many folks know about him. He stays to himself and has very little to do with people. He talks only when he has to. He only comes down out of the mountain to pick up supplies, maybe once every other month or longer. He came in yesterday to get what he needed before the big snow comes. The big snow is what he calls the winter months. Yesterday was the first time he has been off the mountain since before Jason's death. I had completely forgotten about him because his cabin is higher up the mountain than Jason's. Anyway he made a comment to me yesterday, while gathering up his supplies, about a fire in the mountains. He also mentioned something about a metal bird. At first I passed it off because we have fires sometimes high in the mountains. Plus, we have a lot of airplanes traveling around here. Then I got to thinking about Mr. Myland's death. That could have been the fire he was referring to. Anyway, I came to the conclusion a few minutes ago to call the sheriff's office to report it. Let them check out what Indian Joe might know." I eased his mind by telling him to let me check it out first, since the law had already closed the case on Jason. He agreed to my suggestion." he added. Then he told me the only way I could find Indian Joe was to hire a guide. I would have to have different clothes and, of course, hiking boots to make the trip that high in the mountains. Naturally Kayo had all the equipment I would need in his store and at a good price. If I were to make the trip, it would be an all day hike there and back. Sometimes it's an overnight trip. Spending the night in the mountains did not appeal to me. With these thoughts in mind, I asked Kayo to hire me the best guide he knew. He said okay and told me not to worry the guide would be here at 5 A.M. ready to go.

I had gotten so excited about Indian Joe that I had almost forgotten what I had come up here for in the first place. I showed Kayo the photograph of Ginny and asked him if he had ever seen her before. He looked at the photo a long time before telling me "no" but he had seen her picture somewhere before. I told him she had been murdered a few days back. Her photograph had been in all the newspapers. Of course, that must have been where he had seen her. Then I gave him Martha Rogers photograph and asked him the same question. Again he studied the photo, taking his time before answering. He said that this woman could pass for Mrs. Myland's twin. "In fact," he continued, "if she had dark hair I would say it was Mrs. Myland." I had thought the same thing earlier when I met Martha myself. Then Kayo opened the door wide open when he said, "Yes sir, they have the same beautiful light blue eyes; in fact, I think her eyes look better with the light hair than Mrs. Myland's do with the dark hair" replied Kayo. Bingo, it was Martha who came up here with Jason, not Jennifer.

When I arrived at the office, Jean was preparing to close for the day. "I'm glad you are here, Colby," she said. "We have all kinds of things happening today." She related that John had called and said the ball might be in his court, whatever that meant. Only one of the names you gave me to check may be of any significance. John Ray was a personal helicopter pilot for Gilbert Skinner up until a month ago. His mother said that he got tired of what was going on at work and quit. He moved to California. Joan Harrison had called again and left a number for me to contact her. I told Jean she had done well this day and to go home and get some rest, if that was possible.

I called Joan's number but there was no answer. There was no machine for me to leave a message. I will call her tomorrow or the next day. I hung up the phone, got the last cup of coffee and sat down to work for a while. After about thirty minutes, my office door opened. Jennifer, with a big smile, walked in looking like a million dollars. She asked if I would like to take a lonely lady to dinner and maybe dancing. I thought this was not a good time for me to be socializing with my employer, but I had to say "yes". I replied that it would be a pleasure.

I told her I would need to go to my apartment for a shower and shave and to put on fresh clothes. "There's no need to do that" she said. "I know a quaint little restaurant on the south side of Atlanta that no one will know or care who we are and it has excellent food." I said, "Well, what are we waiting for, let's go to the south side."

As we left the office, she said we needed to go in my car because she had come to my office in a taxi. I would have preferred it this way because it makes me feel like I have a date with a beautiful woman. Maybe we are having a date, a real date.

I couldn't help but think about Gilbert Skinner; what would he say if he knew that I was taking his daughter out? Probably words couldn't describe the anger he would have toward me. That's life, ole boy; anyway, it's not his wife I'm out with; it's his daughter.

We arrived at the restaurant; it was very nice and very unique. We ordered dinner and talked about her, about me, and never once mentioned the case. To my surprise, she never brought up Jason or even better yet, she never mentioned Skinner's name. She did tell me that she was supposed to be on her way to New York but just couldn't leave without talking with me. Such a very lovely and lonely woman but if it helps her to talk to me, I will give it my best shot.

Dinner was wonderful, the conversation was stimulating, and the company was awesome. Just being with Jennifer was everything I could wish for; however, when we finished dinner she had changed her mind about dancing. I had blown the chance of a lifetime and couldn't figure out what I had done to make her change her mind. I paid for dinner and we left.

When we got to the car I asked her where she wanted me to take her. I was shocked to hear that she wanted me to take her to my place. I looked at her, and she leaned over and gave me a short sweet kiss on the lips. What heavenly bliss had I stumbled into? I had no idea this would ever happen. After the kiss, I caught my breath and said, "Jennifer, this may not be such a good idea, I mean mixing pleasure with business." I thought how stupid I am to make such a statement like this to a woman like Jennifer regardless of the situation. She looked at me for what seemed like an eternity, then said, "Colby, it has been a long time since I felt about a man the way I feel about you." That was it; all the will power I had was now gone. I couldn't hold back any longer. I leaned over and took her face in my hands and gave her a long passionate kiss. We drove to my apartment, parked in the garage below, and rode the elevator to my floor.

Once inside the apartment, Jennifer wanted to know if I had any type of shirt she could borrow for a while. I went to get number 22, my old high school football jersey. She left for the bathroom while I made us a drink. She asked for bourbon and water. I made two drinks and went to the guest bathroom to shave and shower. After finishing, I put on a pair of jogging shorts and a tee shirt. She was already lying down sipping her drink when I appeared from the restroom. Everything I had visualized about her was true. She looked at me with those beautiful dark eyes that were saying come to me. I was like a lamb, one that was being led to the slaughter by a beautiful goddess. Oh, but what a lovely slaughter it would be. She is more beautiful than I ever imagined. Her hair was down over her shoulders. The numbers 22 on the jersey were standing straight out. Her long, tan, beautiful legs were simply out of this world. All this was about to be mine.

I sat down on the bed and started to kiss her. She stopped me, looked at me with those beautiful eyes and said, "Colby, it has been a long time since I've been with a man, please be gentle." She didn't have to tell me that because she's the type of woman you would want to be gentle with from the very start. I then kissed her very tenderly. I began to find her sweet skin with my fingers, moving them up and down her body. Then the kiss became hard and passionate. I found her breasts; how wonderful they felt. As I took off the jersey, two beautiful mounds stared me in the face. I had never seen such beauty before in my entire life. We continued to kiss with each one becoming longer and more passionate. As we explored each other's bodies, we both began to moan with joy. The moaning and groaning got louder until we finally came together as one. Her fingernails were ripping at my back from sheer delight; it was heavenly bliss. Jennifer might not have had a man for a while but she was by far the best lover I had ever had. It was truly wonderful. Before morning came, we had made love twice. Jennifer wanted to make it three when I told her I had an early appointment. That didn't stop her. We did, and it was more beautiful than the other times and it was worth whatever it may cost me at Kennesaw Mountain.

We both fell asleep. She woke me at 7:15 A.M. telling me she had an 8:25 A.M. flight to New York. We had to hurry in order to make it to the airport in time. She had already showered and dressed and was ready to go. It took me 14 minutes to shower, shave and dress. We got there just in time for her to board her flight. I asked her when would she be back and her reply was, "I will let you know." As she left for flight 192 to New York, she turned and said, "Colby, find Jason for me."

CHAPTER FIFTEEN
Wednesday, December 21, 1988

Jennifer's words, "Find Jason for me," bothered me tremendously. I have never seen her this sure about Jason being alive. What makes her feel so strongly that he is still alive? Is it because she still loves him? If that were the reason how could she have made love to me last night the way she did. Maybe it wasn't me after all; she may have been just lonely, pure and simple.

Upon arriving at my office, I told Jean to find the phone number for Carter's Country Store in Kennesaw Mountain. I needed to speak with Kayo Carter. Within minutes she had Kayo on the phone. "Kayo, this is Colby Grey, I want to apologize for missing my appointment this morning but something came up that was unavoidable. I will make it up to the guide tomorrow. Whatever his fee is per day, I will double it for both days." I asked him if the same time tomorrow would be acceptable and he stated it would. Let me give you my boot size and my clothes size, so that everything will be ready in the morning. After I finished my conversation with him, I told Jean to try Joan Harrison, as I was not able to get in touch with her the night before. I still couldn't place that name or figure out what she might want. Her roommate told Jean that she was a flight attendant and had flown out yesterday for a four-day trip. Her roommate had no idea why Joan had called. She would certainly leave her a note telling her that I had returned her call.

I needed to talk with Kayo Carter again. I didn't think he could help but I had to try. "Kayo," I said, "this is Colby Grey again. You may be able to help me with something else important. Can you describe the steel toed boots and lapel time piece Jason purchased from you in 1983?" Kayo's answer was quick; he told me I could see the catalog tomorrow, since he saves all the catalogs.

Kayo is amazing with his bookkeeping, everything is right in front of him to examine. He may be the one to determine how quickly we solve this case. AND, there is no telling what kind of information I may get tomorrow while talking with Indian Joe.

Let's look at the facts, as we know them at this time. Jennifer did not go to the mountains with Jason. Kayo pointed out Martha as the one with light blue eyes. Jennifer's eyes are dark not light blue. There is no picture in Jason's office for 1983. Jennifer says Jason was in London. Kayo says he and his wife came to the cabin in 1983. Finding the person wearing the right lapel watch will help solve this case. If it is Martha, that will be the proof I need to tie her to Jason. We know she picked up his smoking tobacco at two or three tobacco shops in Atlanta. He always picked it up himself at Kennesaw Mountain.

If my theory about Jason is correct, he was receiving cocaine with tobacco every month. If this is accurate, how was he getting it on the streets? Was he killed because he had been shaving money off the top? Is he dead or alive? If he is not dead then who was in the fire? How many people are linked to his death? If he is dead, does Jennifer know something she's not telling me? Is Gilbert Skinner the brain behind this puzzle? My only hope is that Jennifer knows nothing of the dirty money. All the facts point to smuggling cocaine into Atlanta through tobacco shipments. I wondered if anyone else was receiving tobacco from

Boston? There has to be a connection with someone in the tobacco company. There could be an individual or even maybe a group within the company. Better yet, maybe the whole damn company is involved.

Jean interrupted my thoughts telling me that Gilbert Skinner was on the phone. "Good morning sir, what may I do for you?" I answered. Skinner informed me to be at his office at 11 A.M. sharp. After hanging up, I wrote down a few notes to discuss with John later in the day. I ate a couple of donuts while drinking several cups of coffee. When I finished, I decided it was time to go see Skinner. I would be late by about 15 minutes, simply because he didn't ask me, he demanded that I be there at 11 A.M. sharp. He had not been the one that hired me and with his attitude toward me, I certainly won't cater to him or his demands. As I walked into Skinner's office, his secretary said, "Mr. Skinner is very upset!" My reply was, "He will get over it." She said, "You will find out that he does not like to be kept waiting."

Oh yes, she was right, Skinner was irate. As he began to rant and rave, I was not sure why he was so upset. He began telling me my services were no longer needed. He wanted me off the case as of now. He didn't want me to bother Jennifer or himself again since I had not made much progress toward finding Jason. He thought my fee was too high and was truly a waste of good money. He didn't plan to waste any more money or time with me. He remarked that I had fooled Jennifer, but he was not a female and was not so easily fooled. He was right in one aspect; I had not produced any hard evidence to prove Jason was alive. I still had that inner feeling, however, that Jason was somewhere other than in the ground.

When he finished telling me all he wanted me to know about himself, Jennifer, his money and his power, he proceeded to tell me to get out of his office and not to come back. My reply was, "I will gladly leave with pleasure, but for your information you cannot fire me because you did not hire me in the beginning." I continued, "If I am to be fired it will have to be done by Jennifer, and I am sure if she fired me it would be with class, not like an ass." This remark made him more irate. He jumped from his chair, started toward me, but he stopped when he looked into my eyes and saw I would not bend to his threats. He turned back to his desk almost as fast as he had jumped from his chair; buzzed his secretary and told her that, "Mr. Colby Grey is now leaving." He continued telling her that I would no longer be welcome in the building.

As I left Skinner's office, his secretary gave me the old "go to hell smile." I still couldn't figure out why Skinner was so mad and upset. However, it really didn't matter because I was working for Jennifer. After the night we had, I don't think Daddy Skinner can control her and what she does. Anyway I have too many things to do to worry about his feelings.

I grabbed a couple of low fat sandwiches from Subway on the way to the office for Jean and myself. As we ate our sandwiches, she again told me to be careful of these people for they are dangerous. I told her I would and finished my sandwich.

I called Lt. Black to ask a favor of him. Would he check the files in the drug division to see if Jason had any record of any kind with them? I also gave him John Ray's name just as an after thought. I knew that if there were anything in the files he would find it. He said he would check it out and call me later tonight.

Jean had called Mrs. Ray again, she told her Mr. Ray had entered a contest and was one of the three finalists. It was very important that she contact him and was there a number or address available because he might be the winner of $25,000. At first she said she had no way of contacting her husband, but then she remembered he had called her collect and the number and city should be on the bill. Bingo, again things were looking up for the home team. He was in Fresno, California. Jean also told her not to reveal this information to him or anyone else as it might hurt his chances at becoming the winner of the $25,000. Jean Young, the best secretary in the world, was worth her weight in gold.

Just as she finished and hung up the phone, it rang. It was my investigator, John, in Texas. He had trailed Martha Rogers all day. She had been to the grocery store, to a department store, and to visit an uncle for whom she had purchased the groceries. John had found out that this uncle was the husband of her mother's sister, the one who had been killed in the accident a few weeks ago. There was really nothing else of interest on his part, but he would keep watching her. He would let me know what came of the surveillance tomorrow. Hang in there and we'll talk in the morning was my answer to John.

The day had moved by in a hurry; it was 5:30 P.M. and Jean was getting ready to depart for home. Before she left she put a dinner in the microwave and told me to be sure to eat when it finished cooking. I told her I would and kept right on working. As she left, I reminded her I would not be in tomorrow. My day would be spent at Kennesaw Mountain, hoping that Indian Joe could share something that would shine some light on the case. Maybe he has that puzzle piece that I have so desperately been looking for. I will find out tomorrow, come what may.

I worked until about 8 P.M. Lt. Black had not called and I had been up a long time. I called and left him a message that I was tired and going home. I would talk with him late tomorrow if I got back into town, if not I would call him when I returned. Four A.M. will be here before I know it. Sleep sounds so good.

CHAPTER SIXTEEN
Thursday, December 22, 1988

As I drove to Kennesaw Mountain, my thoughts were not on the case but on Jennifer. I wondered where she was and what she was doing. At this time of the morning, she was probably still asleep. I visualized her lying on the bed with nothing on except my jersey, number 22. Her beautiful tanned body was something every man desired to see and hold. I had been there with her; therefore, I knew that no male could be disappointed with what they found with Jennifer. I certainly was not. My thoughts shifted to Indian Joe as I drove into the country store parking lot. Kayo had everything ready for my mountain trip. I met my guide, changed clothes, put on my new boots, and was ready to hit the trail. Looking at the steel toed boots and lapel pin Jason ordered made me realize this pin was the same pin Martha was wearing. This is a major enlightenment. The guide told me he charged $100 a day, and I had promised him double, so, it would be $400, half now and the rest when we finished the trip. I gave him two $100 bills, then paid Kayo $283 for my clothes and supplies. We were ready to go see Indian Joe.

My guide's name was Sam, and he was excellent. We went in the 4-wheel drive as far as we could, which was about two hours of driving. He had horses ready at a small cabin before we started the major part of the climb. Riding horses is something that I do not do well. But, I knew I had to do it in order to talk with Indian Joe. Another two hours on horseback made my rear sore, but that was as far as we could go on horseback. Sam had another little cabin where we fed and watered the animals and put them in the small stalls to keep them out of the weather. It was another hour to Jason's cabin site and two hours from the cabin to Indian Joe's. There was no way we would be back before dark as it was now pushing 11 A.M. Sam told me we would be back to this little cabin by dark or maybe earlier. We made it to Jason's cabin in 45 minutes so we were ahead of schedule. We did not waste any time there at the burned site because the sheriff's office had done an efficient job combing the area.

Sam was surprised that I was able to keep up with him without complaining about his pace of hiking. We spotted Indian Joe's cabin after another 90 minutes of travelling. We could see who I thought was Indian Joe skinning some kind of animal hanging from a tree branch. The closer we got the more I thought it was a deer, but then I saw it was a wild hog.

Indian Joe saw Sam and me coming up the trail but continued working on his meat. As we approached, Sam shouted out to Indian Joe. Sam told him who I was, what I wanted, and why I had made the trip up the mountain. Indian Joe only grunted and said nothing. This may be a lot harder than I thought but thank goodness I had brought him a good hunting knife and a bottle of bourbon. I offered the gifts and he smiled as he took them. He then asked what I needed to know about his mountain.

Yes, he knew all about the fire and knew what had happened to cause the fire. My reply was, "Great, why don't you tell me anything you know about the fire at Jason's cabin."

He began by telling me that the fire was not caused by lightning but was started by a man and woman. There were two men and they were having a fight. The woman hit the man in the back of the head with the butt of the rifle when he began to get the best of the white man who always brought me firewater. This man and woman went to a small clearing where the metal bird picked him up and flew off. He also told me that the metal bird came many times; in fact, every time the white man came to the cabin, the metal bird came and picked up a big bag from the man. This was the first time anyone went with the metal bird. The woman had gone back down the mountain after the metal bird had left. That was the last he saw of either one of them.

"The white man brought me firewater in exchange for the wild hog I always killed for him." He said. Then he hit me with what I had been looking for all this time he told me the man in the cabin (when it burned) was not the man that always brought him firewater. My instincts were right. Jason is still alive, and Jennifer was right all along. Also, this leaves a lot of questions to be answered. Who was burned in the fire and that makes murder very possible. What does Jennifer know about this because all along she knew Jason was not dead? The big bag must have been cocaine that had been collected during the month. Nice little set up and a smooth operation until something went wrong. The $200,000 had to be dirty money Jason was shaving off the top. I told Indian Joe not to tell anyone what he told me. Also I assured him that he would have firewater each time he went for supplies at Kayo's store, and I would come back to see him as soon as I solved the case. He agreed to do what I asked of him. I knew from the beginning that Indian Joe had some important information to share with me on the case and I was right. I called to Sam and told him I was ready to leave now, hoping to get down the mountain before it was too late. I really needed to get back to Atlanta tonight.

We left Indian Joe's cabin at 1:45 P.M. I told Sam if we could get back to the truck before dark there would be an extra $100 for him. He told me we would make it if I could stay up with his pace. We moved out at a pace that was unbelievable. Of course, getting down was easier than hiking up the mountain. We cut 20 minutes off the time from Indian Joe's cabin and another 10 minutes from Jason's cabin to the horses. After spending very little time getting the horses ready, we were off again. We left on horseback at 3:35 P.M. We were going to make it back to the truck before dark and with time to spare. We fed the horses, put them in their stalls and we were ready to go again.

I drove with caution down the small drive. It took me the full two hours to drive from Sam's cabin to the store. Kayo had already closed but his home was right next door, so it was no trouble for him to open up for Sam and me. We bought a couple of sandwiches, chips and cokes. Man it was good. We ate and talked with Kayo about Indian Joe. I only told him that Indian Joe had been a great help to me but I did not go into details. When we finished eating and talking I gave Sam the rest of his bonus money. He seemed to be pleased with his earnings for the day. I gave Kayo a $100 bill and told him to give Indian Joe a bottle of bourbon every time he came down for supplies. Also, I told Kayo that I would send him enough money to keep Indian Joe supplied with bourbon for a year.

As I drove back to Atlanta, my thoughts were about Jason and where he might be. John will certainly check out everything in Houston because Martha Rogers is an important key to this case. We know that Kayo pointed her out as Jennifer. She knew the way to Jason's cabin. Why did she come with some other man on the day of the fire? There are still many answers I must find in order to solve this case. The answers will surely come with time.

CHAPTER SEVENTEEN
Thursday, December 22, 1988

It took me over an hour to drive back to Atlanta. I didn't realize how tired I was until I parked the car and climbed the stairs. I usually took two to three steps at a time but not tonight. Taking one step at a time was all I could muster. After a hot shower and a strong bourbon and coke, I settled down to watch the news, and the phone rang. It was John in Houston.

He wanted to know if he was to stay with the subject or return home. My first thought was to stay there because Martha might not return to Atlanta, but then I decided against that because he could always go back to Houston. We had a lot to talk about and that overshadowed my original thinking. Of course, he was curious; but he also knew our phones could be bugged. With this in mind, he told me he would see me soon. John was smart and sharp, and I was lucky to have him working for me.

I finished my drink while watching the rest of the news. I was preparing to go to bed when the phone rang a second time. This time it was Jennifer. I was surprised when she said, "Colby, I wanted to call and tell you how much I enjoyed the other night; you are a dear man with a special touch." I told her I felt exactly the same way about her. My next thought was when was she coming back to Atlanta, and I related that to her. Her answer was not a good one. She said that it might be Christmas Day or the day after Christmas before she could complete her business and return. She wanted to know what I had found out about Jason. I told her I had not found him, but I had found some evidence that may tell us why he committed suicide if indeed it was suicide. This was not what she had wanted to hear. I also told her that her father had tried to fire me the day she left, and I had informed him that she had hired me and only she could fire me. I told her we would talk about that when she returned. Again, this was not what she wanted to hear.

We exchanged small talk for about 30 more minutes before we hung up the phone. I could not believe I had talked with Jennifer for over an hour. It seemed as if we had been talking for only a few minutes. It is very easy for me to talk with her. Just talking with her seems to excite me. It may be awful tough for me if we have to wait three days to see one another. With everything she said tonight, the truth is she's the one with the special touch. She is truly some kind of lady.

I turned off the lights and went to bed. I tried to think about the case, but to be perfectly honest, most of my thoughts were about Jennifer. My thinking about Jennifer so much lately is beginning to bother me. Nevertheless, it will not interfere with solving the case.

CHAPTER EIGHTEEN
Friday, December 23, 1988

Getting started today was very easy even though I was a little sore from all the hiking and horseback riding. The reason it is so easy is because yesterday was such a productive day.

Jean was trying to get Lt. Black on the phone for me while I was going over names on the list again, trying to figure out who they were and how they fitted into the puzzle. At least Jennifer's name was not on the list. We knew where Gilbert Skinner, Martha Rogers, John Ray, and Kwee-Un Ji were but Jack Rogers was a mystery as of now. We will find him sooner or later. Maybe we will have at least a little information on some of the remaining five names before Christmas. Facts point to at least two of the five being tied to the tobacco company in some way. My thoughts were interrupted when Jean gave me the phone with Lt. Black on the other end.

I said, "Good morning, how is the fair Lt. today?" Black remarked that he was doing well but would be better after lunch. The information he had for me was not a lot but was important. Jason didn't have a record of any kind in any of their departments. John Ray, on the other hand, had several arrests connected to drugs and robbery. The last one was in 1983 for possession of cocaine. He served four months and was released for good behavior to Jason Myland. That makes me owe Lt. Black one, and knowing him, he will surely collect in the near future. After telling the Lt. thanks for all his efforts, we hung up.

I left the office early with Christmas in mind. I want this trip completed before lunch. Rich's Department Store was my first stop to pick up a Christmas gift for a special lady. Jean would be receiving gold and diamonds this year. Gold earrings with a quarter karat diamond in each earring made them very classy. She will like and appreciate them very much. A visit to a gun shop will find what John wants. A 357-magnum handgun is what he will get for Christmas. He has wanted one like Sara for a couple of years, and now he will have it. John never complains about anything. He never seems to be bothered with work, hours, or travel. Buying the 357 was easy. But John will only get a certificate in an envelope because he has to have the 357 magnum registered himself. Also, he has to be cleared through the State of Georgia before he can actually receive the gun. It's a good law when you try to be selective as to who can own a handgun. Of course, it's not the gun that does the evil, but the person who has control of that gun. Anyway, John will have his 357 shortly after Christmas. He will be pleased with his Christmas gift, I'm sure! That is what Christmas is all about giving to people you care about.

Now I have one more gift to purchase and I have no idea what I am going to get someone who has everything. After much thought, I decided to go to the sporting goods store and purchase a football jersey just like my #22 high school jersey. At least she will know that the other night was a very special night to me. To go along with the jersey, I will send her three dozen red roses, one dozen for each time we made love. Maybe she will understand what I'm trying to tell her. I hope she will realize just how important she has become to me.

When I returned to the office, John had called from
Houston. Jean had checked to see if we were being bugged.
If our line is bugged, there is a light at the bottom of the
phone base that lights up with a blinking red light. Then we
have a password to let the other one know someone is
listening to our conversation. No red light was blinking so
we were safe right now.

John's message was that he would probably be home for
Christmas. He would call later to talk with me about his
findings. He was not sure just how important but he knew it
was significant. Jean said she had no idea when he would
call back. I let her know that it was okay because I would
be there.

The smell of fresh coffee caught my nostrils. Jean sure
knew how to run an office. Coffee, donuts, cake, and other
goodies to go along with her superior abilities as a secretary
made her one of a kind. She takes care of everything,
including me. Efficiency is her middle name.

Art Garrett walked into the office smiling like the cat that
had eaten the canary. Art is one of John's contact men. I
knew he had come up with something good. His smile, his
eyes, and even his walk told me he was proud of what he
had found. He began by telling me that David Shaw was the
hardest to find out about of all the ones they had located.
There were so many David Shaws that fit the description of
the third man, but Shaw is working for a tobacco company
in Massachusetts the T&L Tobacco Company located on
the outskirts of Boston. Then Quinton Coppin, on the other
hand, was rather easy to find. He is the President of the
T&L Tobacco Company. Rodney Day is one of our own
here in the Atlanta Police Department. He works with the

narcotics division, and he is a lieutenant. Joyce Dexter worked for the Building of Glass at one time. She has dropped out of sight at the present, and no one has been able to locate her. Tracy Love has not been located either. Art felt as if it was just a matter of time before all of them were located.

I told Art he and his guys had done one tremendous job in locating these people. Having the knowledge of what he told me will be of great importance in solving the case. One man, Tracy Love, and one woman, Joyce Dexter, are the two we don't know. I wanted Art to tell me how they found these people so quickly. They all had something in common. They had a connection with drugs, mainly cocaine. They were users, pushers, or worked for people who sold cocaine on the streets at one time in their lives. "Art," I said, "John will be back in a few days and will be in contact with you. We appreciate your efforts."

When Art left, I began to go over the notes Jean had typed about each individual. My theory about dirty money was right. Jason was dealing in cocaine. It could have cost him his life, but it didn't because he didn't burn in the cabin. I believe Skinner is the brain behind the operation of the tobacco and cocaine dealings in Atlanta. Skinner had probably put Jason on a hit list for stealing the $200,000. Things were beginning to come together. If Martha was Jason's lover, then she was at the cabin when it burned. She knows who was killed and then burned it to cover it up. She also knows where Jason is and I think I do also.

John will have to go back to Houston or stay there until he finds Jason. I'll bet my car Jason is in Houston somewhere. Everything points to Martha Rogers and Jason being together during this time of his so-called death. Now she is spending more time in Houston than in Atlanta. We just have to find where he is in Houston and then we will solve this case. He is alive but I will not tell Jennifer until we have him.

This afternoon would be a good day to research Gilbert Skinner. Let me review what I already know about him. He is very intelligent, owner of a very powerful company, and never remarried after his wife died. The first thing to check out is to see when the company was started and how the production of the company has grown over the years. My first stop was at the courthouse to check records and deeds. To my surprise, the findings were not what I expected. The computer company was only started a few years back, a couple of years before the death of Mrs. Skinner. Before it became a computer company, it was a textile company owned and operated by Dan Williams. He had organized and put it into operation back in the early 30's. After the courthouse, the library was the next stop on my list. Dan Williams was a textile genius, starting and building the company into a multi-million dollar empire. His wife, Sally Pugh Williams, was the major stockholder when he died an old man in 1960. Dan and Sally had two children, Jennifer Jane Williams, and a son that was still born. Jennifer was six years old when her real father died.

Jennifer told me her mother had died in 1970. It didn't take long to locate Sally Skinner's death as reported in the newspaper. It was one of the largest funerals in Atlanta's history. The article went on to tell her life's history, her marriage to Dan, and then her marriage to Gilbert Skinner in 1963. It reported how her health had declined after Dan's death. Then in March of 1970 Sally Williams Skinner committed suicide by taking an overdose of her medication which had been prescribed by her psychiatrist, A.L. Sanders. Sanders was a life long friend of Sally Skinner. Dr. Sanders needs to be located if he is still living.

After getting all I could from the library, I went back to the office. Jean had left for the day, and she would not be back until December 27. In her note that was left, she reminded me that I was to spend Christmas Day with her family. I wouldn't miss it for the world. She and John are the only family I have since my parents were killed in an automobile accident in Phenix City, Alabama in 1980.

It was pushing 8 P.M. That was the time John said he would try to call. While drinking another cup of coffee and having another sandwich, I waited for John's call. I reread my notes from today, thinking about what a rough life Jennifer must have had growing up. My thoughts continued about Jennifer until the phone rang at 8:30 P.M.; and it was John.

The phone was clean, so I told John about most of the things I had learned in the last two days. I also let him know Martha would sooner or later lead us to Jason. Yes, he is alive if all the evidence I have gathered this week is correct and I believe he is in Houston. I also asked John to stay with Martha and to call tomorrow night about the same time, if possible. "Talk to you then" were our comments to each other as we hung up the phone.

CHAPTER NINETEEN
SATURDAY,DECEMBER 24, 1988

Here I am at the office working the day before Christmas. That's the life of a private detective, especially one with all the evidence I had gathered in the last few days. (I need to fit all these puzzle pieces together) Everyone is gone, John's in Houston, Jennifer is in New York, and Jean is home preparing to have Christmas with her family. It makes me feel strange, like I am alone in the world. Working helps overcome that feeling not so bad; it will help make today a productive one. Time will move quickly if I'm involved in my work. With the office being quiet and no one around will help me get more accomplished.

After I had been working three hours, the phone rang. It was Joan Harrison who had just returned and had seen her roommate's message. She told me the reason she called was she had read that I was working on Jason's case. (It was in the paper that had reported Ginny's murder, that is how she knew I was involved.) She was an old acquaintance of Jason's.

I asked her if she would have lunch with me so that we might talk privately. When she answered, "Yes" we decided to meet in an hour at a small pub named Rocco downtown. After finishing what I was doing, I got my coat, making sure that Sara was in her cradle and was on the way out when the phone rang again. I thought it might be Mrs. Harrison thinking better of a private conversation with me or the voice of some male, but to my pleasure it was Jennifer informing me that she was flying home for

Christmas. Her wish was to see me. Could I pick her up at the airport at 8 P.M. at gate 36? Nothing would give me more pleasure than picking her up at the airport. Just to see her would be a wonderful Christmas gift whether anything else takes place or not. Merry Christmas, Colby Grey.

When Joan Harrison arrived at Rocco's, I knew who she was immediately. She had all the same features Jennifer has, dark skin, black hair and dark eyes. She wasn't blessed with Jennifer's beauty. But then there are not many women who can compare with Jennifer.

We both said "hello" at the same time; she laughed and broke the ice for the moment. She seems to be very nervous. Why did she want to talk with me? What was her connection to Jason? Was it a romantic or business relationship? To give her a chance to calm her jitters, we ordered lunch with wine for her and beer for me. During lunch we made small talk about her work. She really seemed to enjoy flying. You could see the excitement in her eyes when she talked about it. Everything she said about flying was so precise. She drank her wine and sat the glass down. Then she made eye contact with me saying, "Mr. Grey, what I am about to tell you must be kept in the strictest confidence." Her story started by telling me she first met Jason when she applied for a job at the Building of Glass. Jason was a sincere, honest and a hard working man for that company. This was six months before he and Jennifer were married. After his marriage to Jennifer, he changed almost instantly. He became moody, ill-tempered and even began coming to work with alcohol on his breath. His work was no longer important to him. Then he did something that he had continually preached about at every office meeting we had since my employment there. He started smoking. Even though it was pipe smoking, he was using tobacco; and Jason despised tobacco.

He and Jennifer had been married about six months when he asked me to accompany him to a business conference in Chicago. Naive or stupid, she actually thought he needed her for the conference. They checked in to the hotel. Then later, they went to dinner. During dinner Jason drank a lot, in fact he drank too much. When they returned to the hotel, Jason insisted she have a night cap with him.

After a couple of glasses, Jason passed out on the sofa. She covered him with a blanket and went to bed. Some time during the night Jason came to her bed. When she awoke, he had undressed himself completely and partially undressed her. He physically forced himself on her. This was the beginning of their relationship. Whether she had hated him after that or not, it was immaterial because she fell deeply in love with Jason Myland. The relationship lasted almost 18 months. During that time she learned about the dirty dealings in the company. She was like Jason now, caught up in a company with wrong doings. The good thing for her was she was not known by anyone but Jason. By that, no one knew that she knew any thing other than her job duties. She had posed as Jason's wife to pick up his tobacco at a tobacco shop. (She was the other woman picking up the cocaine and tobacco for Jason)

Jason had told her one night that he had forced himself on her because he and Jennifer had not made love since their wedding night. Interrupting her at this point of her story might have been a mistake, but I had to know if he had told her why their marriage had been in such a strain. She only knew that the marriage had been a front for the business.

That's all he ever told her. I ordered another glass of wine, hoping she would continue her story. She found out that she was pregnant with Jason's child. She was afraid for herself and the baby. With the fear she felt, she knew there was only one thing for her to do. Never tell Jason about the baby. This meant quitting her job, changing her name, and moving from Atlanta. She did all three of the above.

Again I had to find out an answer, so I interrupted her. Her answer to my question was very strong and sincere. She did not want anything from Jason or his estate. Her intentions were not monetary but honesty. Her son would know about his father some day, and she didn't want his death to be suicide. She wanted me to find out about Jason's death for her peace of mind. She felt that Jason was murdered because of his hatred for Gilbert Skinner. By that she meant they were always at one another's throat. She mentioned Jason had told her that Gilbert Skinner would have him killed one day.

She looked at me as if she knew what I was thinking. She told me she knew I was working for Jennifer but it could also help her son in the future. That's why she was telling me. A mutual friend had told her she could trust me to do what was right regardless for whom I was working; in fact, this friend told her she could trust me with her life. That made me more curious about our friend, who was he, how did I know him and from where. Again she looked at me for a long moment as if she knew what I was thinking. She met Lt. Black after returning to Atlanta as Joan Harrison and with a deep smile she looked at me, then she said, "My son's real name is Jason Dexter." "Then your name would be Joyce Dexter," I replied. She smiled and nodded yes.

Thanks would never be enough for her coming forward to tell her story. Nevertheless, I told her how much I appreciated her getting in touch with me. As we were leaving, I told her to get in the car, and I would take her home. She told me she had a 3:30 P.M. flight to New Orleans to spend Christmas with her son. So I drove her to the airport. We exchanged small talk about Christmas and families. She told me Jason was looking forward to Santa coming tonight. At the age of 10, he may not have many more of these nights. At the airport, we said our good-byes, wished each a Merry Christmas, and then waved bye.

I returned to the office to see if John had called, but he hadn't. There was only one message, and it was from Jennifer. She wanted me to accept her apology because she would not be able to come home tonight. She did not finish her business in New York. She further explained that she not only canceled her flight, but she also had to cancel the excitement she had built up about returning to Atlanta. She knew the right thing to say to push my button.

I hate Santa won't be bringing me my Christmas present tonight. Oh, what the hell, I have plenty of work to do, especially after what Joan Harrison had just laid on me (or maybe I should say Joyce Dexter). That leaves us with the last name on the list, Tracy Love, a male. We will find Mr. Love, come what may.

CHAPTER TWENTY
SUNDAY, DECEMBER 25,1988

After working as late as I did last night at the office, I slept in on Christmas morning. I knew I had nothing pressing except Jean's Christmas dinner at 6 P.M. After being awake for a few minutes, I ate a bowl of cereal loaded with fresh strawberries. By the time I finished eating, it was 11:15 A.M. I had plenty of time to relax and maybe watch a movie on the tube. Better yet, there will be some pro-football games on television today. This will be an enjoyable day just watching football and relaxing.

I found a game just getting started and believe me when I said I was going to relax, I did just that. I don't even remember the kick-off. The phone woke me at 1:30 P.M. and it was my Christmas present. It was Jennifer calling to wish me a Merry Christmas and to tell me how much she was missing me. After we conversed for a short time, she had to excuse herself. The reason was because she had an early dinner with one of her associates. She did tell me that her business would be finished early Wednesday and that she would return home that afternoon. I told her to let me know what time her flight would be arriving in Atlanta, and I would be delighted to pick her up. After completing the conversation, I realized time was slipping up on me as well.

Arriving at Jean's home with 15 minutes to spare was just perfect. The two youngest children met me at the door excited about their gifts. William was 11 and Susan was almost 10. They had to show me the bicycles that Santa had left. Bicycles today are not like the bicycles we had when we were growing up. Fancy gears and hand brakes make it much easier to ride today.

Jean informed us that dinner was ready. She had prepared a wonderful meal. What I enjoyed the most was the dessert, a German chocolate cake. She had baked it yesterday because she knew it was my favorite. My mother always baked me a German chocolate cake at Christmas. After we finished the feast she had prepared, we retired to the living room. I gave the five children their envelopes, each containing $20. They were proud to receive their money no matter how big or small. Jean was so excited about her earrings that she shed tears of joy. The tears she shed were also for her husband who is a truck driver for PPP Truck Lines of Atlanta (Pride, Patience and Progress) He had a long trip to San Francisco scheduled a little over a week ago. His schedule had him back home by Christmas Day but his truck broke down in California. The repairs were not completed in time for him to get home for Christmas. Thus, he is driving today so he can have his Christmas with his family tomorrow. Jean told me she knew Cory would enjoy and appreciate the tape deck that I had gotten him for his truck.

Jean and I had a glass of wine and talked about the case while her children cleaned up the table and dishes. She has three boys and two girls. Her oldest, Charles is 18, while her oldest daughter, Katrina is 14. Harry the second oldest boy is 16. Her children are well-behaved, especially around other people. That's a good sign that the parents have done a good job of teaching in the early years.

Jean had me a gift certificate from Lee's Gun Shop. She had always wanted me to carry a small weapon for back up, if it was ever needed. That will be my first priority Tuesday morning.

Thanks to Jean and her family, Christmas Day happened to be a good one for Colby Grey.

CHAPTER TWENTY- ONE
MONDAY, DECEMBER 26,1988

There were two messages on the answering machine, both from John on Christmas Day. The first one was at 2 P.M. stating everything was about the same. The second one was at 7:45 P.M. telling me he needed to see me as soon as possible. It must be extremely important for him to want me to fly to Houston. He would be waiting for me at the airport was his last remark.

Calling the airport for the next scheduled flight to Houston was my next move. My flight is at 10:30 A.M. which only gives me an hour to get there. I have a couple of things to take care of before I leave. I must call Jean so she will know where I am. Second, pick up my overnight suitcase that is always ready for such an emergency. Upon arriving at the airport I had to go by the main office to check in Sara. When my flight arrives in Houston, they will return Sara to me. The reason they do this for me is because I have a permit from the Atlanta Police Department; they support my license as a private investigator.

The flight was not a bad flight even though we flew via New Orleans. We arrived in Houston before 1 P.M., which meant we had made good time.

John was waiting for me when the plane landed. We stopped by the main security office to pick up Sara. John had some good news. He believes he has found Jason Myland. Martha led him to Jason. She didn't know John was tailing her when she went to get Jason. Martha is good in trying to cover every aspect of her trail. She took her uncle to an old cabin on the outskirts of Houston. When she left, Jason was with her, not her uncle. Jason had clothes on like the old man so they changed places; Jason was with her now. John told me he had called his friend at the agency in Houston to meet him at the restaurant where Jason and Martha stopped for dinner. His friend picked up the trail there so he could meet me at the airport. John told me his last communication with his friend was over an hour ago and was a very short one. He had trailed Martha and Jason to Monterey, Mexico.

John and I talked about all the puzzle parts that have turned up since he came to Houston. His comment was that everything is falling into place and it won't be long before we solve this case completely. I agreed with him but we still haven't found out where Tracy Love is or what he does. A missing puzzle piece, no matter how large or how small can cause major dilemmas.

As I said, John had spoken with his relief man just before I flew in from Atlanta. They had left Houston taking the I-10 to San Antonio, then to Laredo on Highway 35. They stayed on 35 to Mexico, and then took Highway 85 to Monterey. This is where they are now at a motel in Mexico. We are about nine to ten hours traveling time away from there. Taking turns driving and only stopping for gas, we can possibly make it by 10 P.M. This would be pushing it to the limit, traveling around 500 miles in less than nine hours can be dangerous. We could have flown, but John had checked the flights and none would get us close to our destination.

John drove from Houston to San Antonio in two hours and 40 minutes. We stopped for all the necessities gas, bathroom, changing drivers, food and drink. We were back on the road in 15 minutes. This time I'm putting the pedal to the metal. My time driving was not as good as John's. It took me longer to go the same number of miles. We are running close to five hours and a half in travel time. We arrived in Laredo, a little after 7 P.M. We may be able to make it if the road to Monterey is in good condition. We didn't stop to change drivers; we just kept right on trucking. There were too many questions Jason had to answer to waste valuable time.

When we arrived at the motel in Monterey, the manager told us that John's relief man was in room number five. John knocked on the door, telling him with his special knock who it was. The door opened to a huge man motioning us to be quiet. This man looked to be 6'6", 280 pounds and not an ounce of fat anywhere. He looked like a professional wrestler or pro football player, take your pick. John made the introductions in a low voice; his name was Mark Bush, a very soft-spoken man. He told us they were in the room next to him. He had been listening to Martha and Jason with sophisticated equipment, a glass to his ear and pressed against the wall. There had not been a lot of talking, but there had been a lot of activity since they had arrived here about 10 hours ago. Mark went to the backside of the motel to keep them from slipping out the window. John and I knocked on the door. There was no answer. We knocked again, this time a little harder and then we heard feet moving inside and then heard the window sliding open. Mark yelled, "STOP" in a very loud voice. John ran to the backside of the motel while I stayed at the door. The door opened quickly and there stood Jason in front of me. Even though he had grown a mustache and beard, there was no doubt it was Jason.

I said, "Jason Myland, I am Colby Grey from Atlanta and I have been hired to find you by your wife, Jennifer." He just looked at me, didn't say a word, and just continued staring at me as he stepped back into the room. John and Mark brought Martha in to the room. She was crying. That was the first emotion displayed by Martha at any time during this investigation.

Walking over to Jason, I said, "We need some answers to some questions. That way maybe we can help one another." He looked at me for a long moment, trying to see if I was sincere with my offer. When he spoke he said, "Gilbert Skinner wanted me dead; he hired Jack Rogers to kill me." THEN it was Jack Rogers' remains that were found at the ruins of the cabin fire. Being the hygienist for Dr. Owens made it easy for Martha to switch the dental records. "Jack Rogers made Martha bring him to the cabin, with the intent of killing me, because he knew about Martha and me." He added. They had a vicious fight at the cabin. Jack's head hit a huge rock killing him instantly. It was an accident or self defense according to Jason. When he realized Jack was dead, he planned the suicide death of himself. To cover up the blow to the back of Jack's head, Jason put the rifle in Jack's mouth and used Jack's hand to pull the trigger, blowing the entire back of his head off. The storm and fire was just luck to make it a little harder to prove it wasn't Jason. The story differed from what Indian Joe had told me.

My next question was why Skinner wanted you dead. Then I said, "Jason, we know all about the cocaine ring, how it was sent to you and how you got it off the mountain. We also know about your private safe, your list of names and the money. We want the entire truth from you." Jason stood motionless looking at the floor. When he finally spoke, it

93

was about his beginning work at the Building of Glass; how he was a hard worker and ambitious, wanting to make it to the top of the company. Gilbert Skinner saw this in Jason, and at the time he needed someone he could control completely and Jason was his man. After being there a year, Jason was put in charge of security. This made him one of the big wigs in the company. Then Jennifer came on to him in a big way. Being human, he fell madly in love with her. I almost know that same feeling myself.

He continued his story, telling how Skinner's attitude changed toward him once he started dating Jennifer. Once they were married, he couldn't do anything right for Skinner. It was like he was jealous of Jennifer being married to him. He made numerous calls to her late at night, but when she was gone on a trip or working late at the office he never called. When Jason finally confronted Skinner about calling so late at night, he went into a rage, lost his cool, started cursing and yelling as if he was crazy. Skinner even threatened him with his job and his life. There again, I knew where Jason was coming from. I had been there with Skinner just a few days before. Jason couldn't understand it because he was a good, faithful husband to Jennifer at that time. He went on telling us he was faithful for six months after the marriage. At that time, he discovers that Jennifer has a lover. How did he know this? Deduction! Because he and Jennifer only had sex three times during those six months. Oddly enough all three times were on their wedding night. She seemed to enjoy it then; but that was it, just three times. Jason seemed hurt but this is understandable from a male's point of view.

Then he told me about the tobacco and cocaine smuggling. The cocaine was collected from many cities in Georgia and also parts of Alabama. Skinner got Jason involved without his knowledge of what was actually occurring. Jason was casually asked to pick up his smoking tobacco on several occasions. He even 'persuaded' Jason to start smoking. Then he told him what he was doing and if he stopped helping him, he would turn him over to the police. Skinner was able to hold everything over his head, making Jason get more involved with the cocaine dealings until he was the main collector of the cocaine money. Skinner was able to control Jason because of Rodney Day, the cop in the Atlanta narcotics department who had all the evidence on Jason. Day would put him away for life, according to Skinner. So Jason did what Skinner wanted him to do. The cocaine dealings were worth over a million dollars a week for him.

The money in his private safe came from these collections. He was never able to get to it after the suicide hoax.

QUESTION: Why did you wait this long to leave the United States, and where were you going? Jason's answer was a sincere one or so it appeared to be. He did not have the money, and there was no way of getting any in a hurry. Martha had been working on it everyday since the suicide hoax. His answer on where they were going was very vague. He never really answered it directly.

QUESTION: Who is Tracy Love and what part does he play in this hoax? Again Jason's answer was vague. He only knew the name Tracy Love. Jason was in Skinner's office one day when his secretary called Skinner on the intercom telling him Tracy Love was on the telephone. Jason only heard Skinner's part of the conversation. However, he did remember how pleasant Skinner was talking to him, almost a sweet tone in his voice. The entire conversation was about the tobacco company. Jason assumed it was about the cocaine drops. That was all he knew about Tracy Love.

QUESTION: What part did Jennifer play in the cocaine circle? Jason was almost in a whisper when he answered. The feeling I got from Jason was he didn't want to make it sound as if he was trying to involve Jennifer in any way. She never even talked to him about the tobacco company. Whether she knew anything about it or not, he did not know for sure. There was only one time that made him suspicious about Jennifer's connection with the tobacco company. She was on one of her business trips to New York, but she had taken his cell phone by mistake. When he received the bill there was a call from Boston to Atlanta. He had never been to Boston, so it couldn't have been his call. That didn't sound good for Jennifer's non-involvement in the tobacco/cocaine circle.

QUESTION: What about Joyce Dexter? What part did she play in this cocaine ring? Jason looked at me as if he was shocked and almost shouted, "She was MY secretary, nothing more. She is a loyal person and a very efficient worker. Enough said."

QUESTION: Did Joyce ever pick up tobacco for you? Jason's voice was loud and most defensive when he told me, "NO, NEVER!"

After talking with John we decided to set a trap for Skinner and everyone involved in the cocaine ring. Jason and Martha liked the idea of setting a trap. They were willing to do whatever they needed to do. Mark was willing to take Jason and Martha back to Houston. He would take them back to the cabin where Jason had spent the past few weeks. John and I would return to Atlanta to start the ball rolling on the set-up. If our plan works, we will not only solve the suicide hoax, but we will have broken a tremendous cocaine empire in at least three states. Regardless of what happens, there will be many people arrested by Lt. Black, at the close of this case.

CHAPTER TWENTY- TWO
TUESDAY DECEMBER 27, 1988

On the flight to Atlanta, John and I discussed the possibilities of our plan back-firing on us. We knew that everything needed to work perfectly to pull it off. Also, we knew that Jennifer might be the key to the whole plan. She had to know what we were going to do for a couple of reasons. The most important reason was for me to prove she was not involved with the cocaine ring. The second reason was to find out just how much she would convey to Gilbert Skinner, her stepfather. She has to prove herself to me by keeping everything confidential.

Jennifer was coming in from New York on the 28th of December. That will give me some time to get everything ready. Jean had handled Jennifer's call rather well by telling her that I was following up on a lead at Kennesaw Mountain. She also told Jennifer that it would be late when I returned, but she would see that I received all of her messages. She said, "You can be sure that Mr. Grey will pick you up at the airport when your flight arrives at 8 P.M. tomorrow night at gate 68."

When John and I arrived at the office, I called Lt. Black asking him to meet us at my office as soon as possible. He was there within the hour. Now we could get the ball rolling to close out this case. We all decided it would be best to go somewhere that we knew would be safe to talk and discuss the plan. We agreed once we got outside to go to an all-night diner located on the west side of Atlanta. We knew that anything was possible with Lt. Day being on the force. Every car, apartment and office could very well be bugged. Day could have had everything bugged in the name of the Atlanta Police Department. He could make everything legal by placing me on a wanted list due to suspicion of having information about illegal drugs being smuggled into Atlanta.

The diner was not very busy, so we had our choice of tables. Taking a table in the corner, we could have our privacy and be able to see everyone in the diner.

After explaining the case to Lt. Black, we began to decide how we would go about using the information Jason had given us in Mexico. Needless to say, Lt. Black was shocked at all the information we had gathered about Jason, Skinner, and the cocaine ring in such a short time. His suspicions of Lt. Day had been in his mind for a long time, only now he had some real evidence to prove that he was a dirty cop. All we have to do is prove he is taking drug money from Gilbert Skinner, providing Gilbert Skinner is the head man in the cocaine ring.

At the right time, Lt. Black will contact his friend, a captain in the Federal Bureau of Investigation, to prepare federal search warrants so the raids will be legal at the T & L Tobacco Company in Boston and the Building of Glass in Atlanta. Lt. Black will have Lt. Day working with him at the time it all comes down; therefore, the arrest of Day will be easy. In order for the plan to work the way we want it to, it must all work like clockwork. Perfect timing in all the areas is the key to pulling it off smoothly.

John and I will have Gilbert Skinner covered at the time the plan is put into motion. If Jennifer is involved in any of the cocaine business, I will get her and John will have Skinner. I just hope that I will be going after Skinner myself. That will make me happy and also give me proof that Jennifer is completely innocent of the cocaine ring.

We went over the names of Jason's list with Lt. Black. We knew where Jack and Martha Rogers, Kwee-Un-Ji, Gilbert Skinner, David Shaw, Quinton Coppin, Rodney Day, John Ray, and Joyce Dexter were; but then there was one name, Tracy Love, that we had not located. Tracy Love made the tenth name on the list; but no one knew anything about him, not even Jason. All Jason knew was the name. If Tracy Love can be found, we will find him; it's just a matter of time.

After we finished everything, deciding where, how and when we were going to pull this off, we all agreed that I would make the final decision as to the exact time to begin. The plan was a good one, but only time will tell whether it can be pulled off successfully or not.

Upon arriving at my apartment, I found I had two messages on my answering machine. One was from Jennifer telling me how much she had missed me, and she could hardly wait to see me tomorrow night. Then the shocker came when she said, "Colby, I think I'm falling in love with you." That statement I had not counted on. This could really complicate my part of the plan knowing how I feel about Jennifer and now knowing that she loves me. The second call was from Joan Harrison telling me she needed to talk with me on the 28th. Joan said she would arrive in Atlanta around 11 A.M., and she would like to meet me around noon at the same pub we had lunch before.

Even with the statement of love from Jennifer and knowing my feelings for her won't stop me from solving this case. The possibility of her being involved in the cocaine ring is greater today than it was three days ago. I truly hope that I am wrong on that assumption. My promise to Ginny as she lay on the cold tile floor of Jason's shower was to find and punish those responsible for her death. That promise will be kept no matter how much it may hurt me or any one else.

CHAPTER TWENTY-THREE
WEDNESDAY, DECEMBER 28, 1988

After a good night's sleep, one that was needed very badly, I was ready for a day at the office. I arrived about 8:30 A.M. Jean had the coffee ready as usual, but this morning was special. She had made some of her good buttermilk biscuits, stuffed with sausage. Her biscuits are the best I have ever tasted. It's always a treat when she brings them to the office. After having one of her treats, I had to know what the special occasion was. Her answer was that she was glad I was home safe and sound. That was very thoughtful of her. I thanked her for being such a wonderful secretary.

By the time the second sausage and biscuit was gone, John came in with a bag of donuts. Of course everyone in the office had to have a donut. All this eating this morning will take care of lunch for me. Water and salad will be all I can have with Joan today. My mind began to drift, wondering what she had forgotten to tell me at our last meeting. Oh well, she will tell me at lunch. There's no need trying to figure it out now. It must have seemed very important for her to call me from New Orleans. Hopefully the information will be of some help to our closing out this case. Everything is welcome when it comes to solving a case.

We made a call to Mark in Houston and everything was fine. Jason and Martha were ready to set the plan into action. I asked Mark to tell them that it may be a couple of days before we would be ready on this end, but we would keep in touch. Just tell them to sit tight and be patient; the right time will come soon enough.

By the time we finished talking with Mark, it was time for me to go to Rocco's to meet Joan. I actually arrived about 20 minutes early. Thank goodness I did arrive early because I spotted two of Atlanta's finest waiting outside the pub. There was not enough time to get in touch with Joan so I would just have to wait. Knowing that I took her to the airport before she left for New Orleans gave me the edge. That probably meant she would be coming in a cab. Getting to a phone, I called the airport and spoke with the personnel director. I found out Joan's flight had come in about 15 minutes ago. Joan had already left the airport for a lunch appointment. I told the director I was the one she was to meet for lunch and I needed some help. I asked her if she would call Joan and tell her we have to change our meeting place. She said she couldn't do that, but then she said her supervisor might be able to help. After explaining the situation to the supervisor, she said she could get in touch with Joan in a matter of minutes. I gave her the phone number from which I was speaking so she could call me back after talking with Joan. It seemed as if I waited for an eternity, but finally the phone rang. It was Joan. Of course, she wanted to know what was going on. I only told her she could not go to Rocco's. I found out where she was and how long it would take her to pick me up at the street behind the pub. Approximately five to 10 minutes was the estimation, and it was now 12 minutes after the hour. Cell phones are worth their weight in gold. At least this time it was worth much more, maybe Joan's life.

We went back to the airport exchanging small talk about our Christmas holiday. She told me all about her son and what he had gotten for Christmas. When we arrived at the airport, I paid the driver, tipped him heavily, and told him to forget about us. He smiled, then said he had never seen us. We went to a private room next to the personnel director's office. After talking with the personnel director a few minutes, we had decided to send Joan back to New Orleans. I also told Joan to call her father and explain that there may be danger to the entire family. Her father was to pick her up at the airport and go somewhere safe for a few days. I also explained that this could be a hoax, but for their safety, we needed to carry this out. With all the essentials taken care of for Joan and her family, the pressure on me didn't seem so intense.

As we waited for her flight to New Orleans, Joan began to tell me what she had forgotten to tell me during our first meeting. Actually she didn't forget, just didn't think it was important until she began to think about it during Christmas.

She began by telling me of a conversation she had overheard in Ginny's office. She was working in Jason's office when she heard Ginny crying. Joan had moved closer so she could see Ginny and whoever it was that made her cry. She was talking to someone on the telephone. Of course, she didn't know whom she was talking with in the beginning; but she found out later as she listened to the conversation.

Hearing only Ginny's part of the conversation helped. It went something like this: "But I don't want to see him outside of work.... pause...... yes, of course I will, you know my love for you is real ..... pause ..... yes, I will tell you everything that happens..... pause ..... yes, yes, even the intimate feelings that we have with one another ..... pause...... of course, I will, yes I promise on my love for you." Then there was a long pause and Ginny said, "Jennifer, my love for you is real and no matter what ever happens I will keep you informed about everything." .... Pause..... "yes, especially about sex and work." Ginny hung up the phone crying a little harder and louder. Joan went back to Jason's desk, continued working until Ginny went to the restroom. Then Joan left Jason's office and went to her own.

Joan said she assumed later that they were talking about Ginny and Jason. The reason for her assumption was Ginny began to take the edge of work off and became more friendly to Jason. Before, she had been very straight laced; it was work and nothing but work. Jason told Joan on several occasions, after she heard the conversation, that Ginny was being very nice to him, beyond the work duty requirements. Joan never told Jason about the phone conversation. Joan found out she was pregnant shortly after Jason told her about Ginny, that is when Joan left Atlanta.

Looking at Joan with a face of amazement, I didn't' know what to say. Ginny was gay or bisexual! Does that mean that Jennifer is gay or bisexual? Of course, that is exactly what it means. If this about Jennifer and Ginny is true that is how Jennifer knew about the money in Jason's office safe before I told her. Ginny had told her everything, about the list, the safe, the money, and probably about me. She knew everything before I picked her up at the airport. Jennifer is a very cool and smooth woman.

Joan had a puzzled look on her face; then, I assured her that this was very important for me to know and she had done the right thing by telling me. This has answered several questions. In fact, it might be just what we need to solve this case. Taking her face in my hands, telling her I might have some good news for her in a few days, brought a smile to her face. Just then the captain came and told Joan it was time to get started. Joan departed into the director's office for a few minutes. When she returned she was several years older with gray hair, glasses, and a larger bust line. Very good disguise, Ms. Harrison, very good indeed. I asked Joan if she had Lt. Black's office number. She said she did and that she would call him when she was settled in New Orleans. To verify that you are talking to Lt. Black, tell him this is Shayna, then if indeed it is Lt. Black he will say Shayna Price. Price is your key word. "Good luck, that really is a good disguise," I said as she left the office.

I remained in the personnel director's office, watching the plane depart and thought about what Joan had said. This is one more mixed up case. Some of the things I am beginning to find out are getting close to MY feelings. That's my own fault because the first law of a private investigator is to never get involved personally with your case or anyone involved in the case.

It was about 2 P.M. I needed to call Jean to find out the day's events and also to see if I had been missed. Jean told me that nothing of importance had happened but Ms. Sara Parker came by to see me. I told her you were not taking any new cases at the present. Password Sara, so our office phones are bugged as well as my apartment phones. I told Jean I would see her before she went home tonight. That was my last statement before I hung up.

I went straight to the office, arriving there before 3 P.M. Jean wrote several notes on a pad for me to read. (1) John would see me around 5 or 5:30 P.M. (2) She had made me an appointment with Dr. A.L. Sanders at 4 P.M. (Dr. Sanders had been retired since the mid 70's) (3) Lt. Day had called earlier today, around 1 P.M. (4) She had written down Dr. Sanders address. I motioned thanks and left for Dr. Sanders' place.

Arriving at Dr. Sanders' apartment at the exact time he wanted me was perfect. He welcomed me in and asked how he could be of assistance to me. I explained who I was, what I was doing, and how he could help me. I also told him I understood how his confidentiality might keep him from disclosing any information to me because I had the same problem disclosing information about my clients. He examined me for a few minutes, then walked over to the phone and dialed someone's number and waited for an answer. "Hello, Blake, this is A.L. I have a favor to ask of you. Do you mind helping me? Okay, here it is. Do you know a private investigator by the name of Colby Grey? You do, okay, what kind of man is he? Can we trust him to be an honest man? Okay, so you think he will do what he says he will do. Okay, you bet. Thanks Blake, talk to you later. By the way, see you tomorrow night at the game."

Dr. Sanders hung up the phone, turned to me saying that he was talking to Blake Sinquefield, one of the greatest legal minds in the country. "He is the best sitting judge on the bench today in the United States. He says you're okay, that you are an honest man, a man of integrity, and one that can be trusted. Even with all the good things he said about you I couldn't tell you what you want to know. My confidentiality must be unconditional to my clients even if they are dead and I am retired." I arose from the chair telling Dr. Sanders thanks for his time. I could certainly appreciate and understand his decision. As I shook his hand he said, "You know my file cabinet with all my closed files are in the den. I'm going upstairs to shower, shave, and get ready for dinner. So Mr. Grey, will you excuse me for about 30 minutes?"

Finding Sally Pugh Williams' file was very easy, as it was located at the back of the second drawer. She had major problems with life after her son was stillborn. This was when she started seeing Dr. Sanders. Her problems increased when her husband, Mr. Williams dies. She was afraid of life because of her insecurities. When she met Gilbert Skinner and started dating him, things began to change. Dr. Sanders had stated she felt a little more secure about herself and life. After that for about three years or so she only came to see Dr. Sanders when she wanted to or felt the need to do so. Things seemed to be going well for her. Then in 1967 she became insecure again. It got worse each year until 1969, and then she related to Dr. Sanders what had happened to destroy her life. Gilbert was having an affair right in front of her in her own home. She never told Dr. Sanders with whom he was having an affair with but it was someone in the house and that hurt her deeply. Then in 1970 she took an overdose to end it all.

As I was replacing the file in the cabinet the sound of footsteps appeared in the hall. Meeting Dr. Sanders at the door, I extended my hand and told him I had to leave and that it was my pleasure to have met a gentleman like him.

When I returned to the office, John had been waiting awhile for me Jean had gone home for the day. I motioned for John to go. Getting outside, I told John I had to go to Rocco's to get my car. Time was running out, and I had to pick up Jennifer at the airport at 8 P.M. On the drive to Rocco's, I

Come What May, Colby Grey

filled John in on all that had happened today. John remarked, "You had a busy day. It sounds as if Jennifer is a user of people." That statement bothered me because I had already thought that myself.

As I got into the car, I had to hurry; I needed to go to the apartment to shower and change before picking up Jennifer. My thoughts were in a turmoil. This may be the beginning of the end with this case. Whatever happens tonight with Jennifer could mean the end is closer than I think.

CHAPTER TWENTY-FOUR
WEDNESDAY, DECEMBER 28, 1988

Jennifer's plane was 20 minutes late when it landed. I was ready to see her whether she was involved in the cocaine ring or not. In fact, I wondered how I would react if she were guilty. The feeling I have for Jennifer is like none I've ever had before. I just hope she is not involved, but if she is then I will have to handle it some way.

All of a sudden she appeared at the doorway. Oh my world! She is a beautiful woman. Her smile began to widen as she got closer to me. Then we were in one another's arms, kissing like we had been lovers for years. Finally, when the long kiss ended, she looked at me with those beautiful eyes that seemed to be saying, "I want you." Then, she finally spoke, saying, "Colby, you don't know how much I've missed you." She continued, "I can't wait for us to talk; there is so much we need to discuss. There has been a lot of time on my hands while in New York; the time gave me a chance to re-evaluate my life." Then she stopped, looked at me, and kissed me again. After the kiss, she said, "Yes, Colby, I love you. I didn't mean for it to happen, it just did and I couldn't help myself." At this time, I spoke for the first time, telling her she was having post-Christmas blues. Being away from home at Christmas time always gives you the blues. She looked at me with disappointed eyes. Those big dark eyes began to swell up with tears. That was something I could not stand. I said, "Jennifer, I don't know whether it's love or not, but you have been with me in everything I have done since you left. If that, combined with wanting to hold you, kiss you, and make love to you is love then I'm in love too." This brought a smile to that beautiful face of hers. Only being in love one time before, I couldn't honestly say whether I was in love with her or not. I know the feeling is not the same as it was with Sara Mandell.

We walked and talked but not once did she mention Jason. She was telling me all about the meetings she had to attend during her stay in New York. When we picked up her luggage and moved toward the car, it was almost 9 P.M. and she still had not mentioned anything about the case. This puzzled me a little; maybe she was in love with me and all else didn't matter.

As we drove toward downtown Atlanta I asked her if she had eaten dinner. She said "No," but what she would like to do was to grab something quick so we could eat it on the way to my apartment. That suited me, so we pulled into a drive-in and ordered two chicken sandwiches, french fries and cokes. We ate them on the way to my apartment. It had been a long time since I enjoyed my sausage and biscuits this morning, so I was ready for food of any kind including fast food. We continued talking as I drove, but Jennifer never mentioned the case. Then I finally broke the ice by telling her that the case was going well. We had come up with a lot of information during the Christmas holidays. She said nothing at this time, just kept eating her fries. Finally she spoke, saying the case was one of the things she wanted to talk with me about. She said, "Colby, I have no desire to find Jason any more. This may sound heartless to you, but I don't care anymore. I told you I love you. I don't want you to find him even if he is alive." She continued saying that her real problem would come tomorrow morning when she goes to see Gilbert. Then I asked, "Why should that be such a problem: He's only your stepfather and maybe a partner in your business." Jennifer stared into the darkness of the night before speaking as if she was trying to choose the right words. Finally, breaking the silence she said, "There are a lot of things you don't know about my family and if you did you would not understand. I hope that you will never find out; and if you do, I'm afraid you won't understand about the dirty details surrounding my life. Please don't ask me to tell you. I love you; but I won't tell you, not now, maybe years from now I will, but not now." She was now crying, and I felt guilty for some reason. To ease my pain, I reached over and touched her leg, giving it soft squeezes as if I was saying don't worry about it, Jennifer. I certainly won't let it interfere with our relationship. I felt as if I knew already what she was speaking about. She didn't have to tell me about the cocaine ring and her involvement. If that's all she is worried about, we can work that out if she really wants to.

We took the elevator up to my apartment floor. When we stepped out of the elevator, there was Gilbert Skinner waiting for us. He was red in the face (a great deal redder than the day in his office) when he asked, "Jennifer, just what in the hell do you think you're doing?" Jennifer answered "Gilbert, what are you doing here? You need to go home; I will see you in the morning at the office." He replied, "To hell you will, you're coming with me right now." That was my cue to step in between them telling Skinner that Jennifer, not him, would make that decision. If she wanted to go with him she could; but, on the other hand, if she chose to stay with me she could do that also. That's when he said, "Okay, Mr. Colby Grey, you asked for it. Fellows, take care of our pretty boy here." I have been called a lot of things but never pretty boy. Three big men stepped out from around the corner of the hall. As they were walking toward me Jennifer said, "Okay, Gilbert, you win." I told Jennifer that she did not have to go that I could handle these three goons. She told Skinner she would go with him, but if they touched me he would regret it. She said to Skinner, "I promise you, you will regret that decision." Skinner motioned to his goons; they got on the elevator with Skinner and Jennifer. The door closed with Jennifer telling me with those big dark eyes that she was sorry.

I opened the door to my apartment, went in and sat down on the sofa. What had just happened was proof that Jennifer had done a lot of soul searching. I feel she has made up her mind what is important to her. She was provoked into doing what she just did. Also, she saw me reach up and put my hand on Sara when those goons started toward me. I'm sure she didn't want anything drastic to happen. That's the reason for her actions.

This may put a hold on activating our plan for a short time.

CHAPTER TWENTY-FIVE
THURSDAY, DECEMBER, 29,1988.

The phone rang at 7 A.M. It was Jennifer telling me to meet her for breakfast at Bill's Kitchen at 8 A.M. I told her I knew the location of Bill's, and I would be there. Then I asked her if she was okay. She replied that she was fine. After hanging up the phone, I showered and shaved, then went to the car.

At 8 A.M., I was at Bill's Kitchen waiting for Jennifer. She walked in a couple of minutes later looking like royalty. She saw me and started toward me with a big smile on her face. She was radiant looking even in the morning. She sat down while apologizing for last night. She told me that Gilbert was a very protective man especially since Jason did what he had. I didn't say a word; just let her do the talking while I listened. Jason had several affairs in the first few months of their marriage. Jason and Gilbert had trouble from the time the affairs were known. Jennifer said, "A divorce could have solved the problem, but I loved Jason, or at least I thought I did. Now I'm not so sure because the feeling I had for him is not the same as I have for you, Colby. With a divorce, there would have been a scandal to go along with it, so I never pursued a divorce." She went on telling me that Jason was mixed up with some suspicious people. Every time she or Gilbert would question him about it, he would get upset and storm out of the office. He used poor judgment on several occasions. He hired a man by the name of Ray that had been in prison, and had also hired another man by the name of Rogers that proved to be an outlaw. Jason had been entrusted with one of the most important facets, the security of the firm; however, he demonstrated poor judgment when he hired these two men.

She stopped talking, opened her purse and handed me a check. When I looked at the check, she spoke, "That should be enough to cover the days and expenses." The check was for $12,000. Two thousand of the $12,000 was for expenses. Looking at Jennifer, I finally spoke telling her we had not solved the case yet even though we were getting close. Then I asked her if she was sure she wanted to fire me at this time before we found Jason? She looked at me and said, "I don't care whether Jason is alive or dead. I'm sorry but I just don't care. Colby, I'm not firing you, I just feel it's best for everyone concerned to stop the investigation." My response to that was if that's what she wanted, I would package all the evidence and get it to her. It may take a couple of days, but she would get it as soon as possible. Then we ordered our meal. While we were waiting for our food, we talked about our relationship and what we expected of our relationship. She wanted us to continue seeing each other. Of course, I agreed with her; it was a great idea. I thought to myself, "Well, Skinner you won the battle but you haven't won the war." He had convinced Jennifer that there was no need in continuing my employment.

I had not counted on this happening. It just might mean I need to speed up things a bit. The trap has to be set at the right time or it won't work. While I was thinking, I could hear Jennifer talking, but I was not listening. Then I heard her asking me where was I, that I had not heard a word she had said in the last five minutes. I told her I was sorry but I was thinking how fast I could get everything together for her. Our breakfast came, so we talked very little as we ate. When we finished, I paid the bill and we walked outside. Her car was sitting there with her chauffeur opening the door for her. She got in the car and then turned toward me and said, "I will be looking for your report soon." She blew me a kiss from the window as they drove away.

The time was 9:25 A.M. and my next stop was the gun shop where Jean had purchased my gift certificate, and had taken care of all the arrangements. They had everything ready when I went in the shop. The character check had been returned from the state and all I had to do was pick out the weapon I wanted. I chose a small .38 special with a leather holster, one that I could strap to my leg and it would not be seen. I got a box of cartridges, put five in my special as that is all it holds. I decided that I should purchase a cartridge holster for the other leg. That would give me 10 cartridges in the event they were needed.

When I got to the office, I found it was locked but the coffee was hot. Jean had left me a note on my cup telling me she had gone to the bank and to the post office to pick up a package for me. Who would be sending me a package? What could it be? The red lights began to blink on and off in my mind. Having a suspicious nature is what has helped me in my profession. It was certainly working now; however, I knew Jean would not open the package and there was no need to worry.

When I got my coffee poured, John walked in with Jean; and they were conversing. What a relief it was to see them both. I motioned for both of them to come into the hall. We talked for a few minutes and every once in a while I eased the door open and told Jean to bring me something containing the Myland case. I told them what had happened last night as well as what happened this morning. John said, "You are right about these people, Jean." We all agreed

116

with that statement. We then went back inside to check out the package. It did not have a return address and had been mailed in Atlanta. We decided we would not open it in the office. Maybe there is nothing to it, but I had rather be safe than sorry.

John and I decided to take the package to the shooting range. The range has a bomb room, which contains an apparatus with mechanical arms that can open packages. John had done this before, so he was elected to operate them. The arms began to remove the wrapping paper with John's guidance. Finally, all the paper was gone, then the arms began to open the box. As the arms opened one side of the box there was a tremendous explosion. I was not surprised one bit. After the smoke cleared, we began collecting bits and pieces from the explosion.

We stopped at the first pay phone to call Lt. Black. I told him what had happened and that I thought we might need to get together. He agreed with me, and we set a time to meet at the diner. I also asked him if Shayna Price had called him in the last 18-20 hours. His answer was affirmative which made me feel good. Now that we know she is safe, we can move ahead with our plan. We now know that we have put the fear of God in Skinner's cocaine outfit. We are certain they know we are on to their cocaine trafficking.

When we returned to the office, I remembered I had not given John his Christmas present. I gave him the certificate for a .357 magnum. John was just like a child, so excited! He had to go to the shop right then; he couldn't wait. When John left, I showed Jean the present she had given me. She was very pleased with my selection. It gave me a second gun in case of an emergency.

Johnny A. Sanders

I worked in the office until 5 P.M. John had returned from the gun shop, telling me he could get his gun tomorrow. Since he was a certified gun owner already the check wouldn't take the required time limit. Jean was leaving for home as John and I finished the final touches on the report to be given to Jennifer. Then later tonight we will meet with Lt. Black.

CHAPTER TWENTY-SIX
FRIDAY, DECEMBER 30, 1988

On the way to the office I thought about Jennifer and how beautiful she was coming toward me in the cafe yesterday. I may be wrong, but I believe she was sincere when she said she loved me. Her concern was for me the other night, when confronted by Skinner and his three goons. I could see Jennifer's concern in her eyes. There is no doubt that Jennifer is very important to me. My wish is that my thoughts about her loving me are correct. I have to call her today so maybe we can have lunch. I want to tell her about the bomb that I had received. I want to read her expression, to see if I can discern if she had previous knowledge of the package in any way.

Jean had all the usual things done, coffee made, donuts ready and she had written three notes for me. She had also motioned for me to be quiet as I came in. The notes she gave me were from Jennifer, Lt. Black and Lt. Day. Lt. Day calling me means Lt. Black had put the plan into motion. That would be the only reason for him calling. Jennifer left a phone number I was not familiar with, and I can usually remember numbers, but not this one.

Jean brought me a cup of coffee and a donut. I wrote her a note telling her I was going to the drug store to use the pay phone. She smiled and nodded okay at the same time. As I drank my coffee and ate my donut, I looked at the phone number Jennifer had left. I had never used this number to call her before at any time. I had put several question marks by Jennifer's number when Jean saw what I was doing. She took my pen and wrote me a note on my desk pad. It's her cell phone number, Colby. This time I looked at her, and nodded as if to say thanks and I understand. I left the office giving her the thumbs up sign indicating a job well done.

When Jennifer answered her phone, I told her not to mention my name. "Just listen and answer my questions, do you understand?" I said. She replied that she did understand by saying yes and I do. I asked her to meet me for lunch and again she replied, "Yes." Then we decided upon 12 P.M. at Billy's Kitchen. She added something about a dress fitting and that she would be in a little before lunch.

Then I called Lt. Black but he was in a meeting with Captain Jones and would be tied up for a while. Since I didn't get a chance to talk to Lt. Black, I put Lt. Day's call on hold until after lunch.

I was putting Jennifer to a test, and I'm sure she knew it from the beginning. I only hope she shows up by herself and not with Skinner or his goons. The bit Jennifer used about a fitting for a dress before noon was great. If she is sincere about me, there will only be the two of us having lunch at Billy's today. Maybe my sixth sense had correctly identified her feelings for me. Only time will tell me what I am looking for from her. I definitely hope so anyway.

Upon returning to the office, I found John; so we went outside to talk. I told him what had transpired this morning and he only looked at me and shook his head. Then he said, "Colby, I can't believe you are doing this to yourself." He paused for a few seconds and then told me he would be near Bill's Kitchen in case I needed him. I thanked him and we went in the office to have a cup of coffee. This time I spoke to Jean and she told me about my calls. I made like a busy beaver calling Jennifer's number first. Thank goodness I got her answering service. The message I left her was about the paperwork on the case. I told her I had not gotten it all together as of yet, but it would be in her hands by tomorrow. Then I told her how much I was missing her before I told her good-bye.

Then I called Lt. Black again, but this time he and Lt. Day had gone to lunch. I looked at my watch and it was already 11:15 A.M. I worked for another 15 minutes before asking John if he wanted to join me for lunch. It will take around 20 minutes to get to Bill's from the office and that will give me 10 minutes extra to settle in before her arrival. She is always late. Jennifer likes to make a grand entrance for our appointments.

Time wise, I was right. I got to Bill's 10 minutes before the hour. Jennifer walks in with a big smile coming straight to me. I smiled back. As I arose from my chair to greet her, I thanked her for coming because I needed to have a talk with her. Her first remark was "Colby, you were testing me this morning and I'm not sure that I like that at all." I looked at her and said, "I was, but first let me explain why I did what I did. After our meeting for breakfast yesterday morning, I received a package from someone here in Atlanta. If we had opened it in the office, Jean and I would have both been killed and there's no telling how many other people in the building would have been injured or lost their lives. It was a very powerful bomb. I studied her reaction to what I had said. She looked straight at me with tears in her eyes and said, "You think I had something to do with sending you a bomb?" My answer was, "No, but someone wants me dead and I think we both know who that someone happens to be." Reading her eyes had told me what I wanted to know. She was totally shocked about the bomb and the hurt in her eyes showed me she really cares for me. She told me that she had a long talk with Gilbert just this morning about me. "He really hates you," she said. She continued and explained that the reason he hates you so much is because he knows I love you and he can't stand the thought of me loving anyone. I looked at her straight in the eyes and said, "I love you, too."

We ordered lunch, talked about our relationship and how we are going to settle this problem with Skinner. She told me that she had to go on a trip to Florida with Skinner tomorrow and would be gone for at least a couple of days. They would be flying in his private jet to a small fishing town in the panhandle of Florida. Destin, Florida, was their destination. Destin has a small airport, but there are many planes coming and going constantly. She also related that Destin has a good-sized fishing harbor and docks. The thought occurred to me that that maybe this is the way they get their cocaine into the country. Drugs being smuggled in on fishing boats! This wouldn't be the first time this had happened in the United States.

I asked Jennifer when she was leaving for Florida. Her reply was this afternoon around 3 P.M. She told me she hated to fly in that small jet of Skinner's, and she was not very fond of his flying skills either. That is why she said she always tries to fly commercial but not on this trip. She also related that they own a condominium at Gulf Terrace, right across the street from the airport which is easily accessible after their flights in from Atlanta. She then looked at me seriously with sad eyes and told me she would be staying in Destin the next couple of nights.

When we finished our lunch, she and I bid farewell again for a few days. She would be in Florida for the next couple of days and so would John and I. That means there is a lot to do between now and the time we leave. The first thing was to find a Florida map to see just where Destin is located and how long it will take us to get there in case we have to drive.

John called a friend of his at the airport in an effort to find out Skinner's flight plans. Finally after holding the line for 15 minutes, John learned that they were to take off at 3:30 P.M. The only flight to that part of Florida we could find was a Delta connector to Panama City, Florida. Destin is about an hour driving time from Panama City. Jean will have us a rental car ready at the airport when we land and we should be in Destin by 4:30 P.M. That will be just about the time Jennifer and Skinner will be arriving at the airport.

When we landed in Panama City, we were a few minutes behind the schedule I had set up earlier. It was 3:45 P.M., and we had to rush to get our transportation. Jean had taken care of everything, so all we had to do was sign for the car. They even had the car (actually it was a van) ready at the front of the airport. We were on our way in 10 minutes after landing. John had talked with the car agent about the best route to Destin, while I was signing for the car. We had mapped out our route from Panama City to Destin --- easy, stay on Highway 98 all the way to Destin or about 60 miles straight ahead on Highway 98.

John drove the first part of the trip while I worked on my disguise. Our disguises had to completely fool Jennifer and Skinner in case they see us while tailing them. I will appear to be much older, have longer gray hair, and be sporting a full beard. I will also have a bad scar running from the outer part of my left eye to my nose. I have a set of contact lenses that change the color of my eyes. Oh yes, I will have a small hump on my back. By the time I finished my disguise and changed clothes, we were in a small beach community called Santa Rosa Beach. John had been driving hard for about 40 minutes. We stopped long enough for me to run around to the driver's side. While I drove, John worked on his disguise. He will appear to be rougher, have a straight pointed nose, rough beard, and he plans to wear an eye patch. He did look like a rough customer. We were about 15 minutes later getting to the airport than we had planned.

We parked the car, went inside to see what flight had come in the past hour. We were amazed even more when we saw all the flights on the board that had come and gone today. There had been only two flights in the past hours, one from Tennessee and the other from South Carolina. There was one from Atlanta due to arrive at 4:30 P.M., but had been delayed in Atlanta because of a thunderstorm.

John and I went back to the car to wait for Jennifer and Skinner to arrive. After about 10 minutes we heard a plane and saw it coming in for a landing. The plane landed then taxied to a spot where an attendant showed the pilot a parking space. Two people emerged form the plane walking toward the airport terminal. It was Jennifer and Skinner. I could spot Jennifer's walk from anywhere. They were in the terminal for only a few minutes before they reappeared. There was a car waiting; they got in and drove off. John and I followed them to the entrance of the condominium complex, which was only a short distance from the airport. When they turned in, we continued down Airport Drive but quickly turned around and continued our following. There would be no suspicion of someone following them now because we were far enough behind them not to be noticed.

They drove around to the opposite side of the entrance to building #20. Skinner parked the car and then went up the stairs to the second floor. We saw the lights on in unit number 2005.

At this time of the year it is dark at 5 P.M. and it was past 5 now. John and I talked about how we would handle our surveillance operations, which of us would take the first watch and so on. We knew they would probably go out to eat at some point but when and where was the question. Great, about that time the lights went out in 2005 and that means they are not going to waste any time. We followed them as they turned right on Highway 98 driving to a restaurant called The Flaming O Restaurant. John and I drove on to the next street exit, turned around and went back; parking in an area across the street in a small shopping center. They were in there around two hours, having an elegant dinner we assumed. Once they left the restaurant they drove to the harbor where they parked and walked down to the docks and specifically to a fishing boat called The Dolphin Queen. Both went aboard and disappeared for about 30 minutes. John and I had gotten close enough to the Queen to see them and hopefully close enough to hear the conversation from within. We did hear some conversation from Skinner, "You'll get the rest when our man comes tomorrow." The captain didn't sound disappointed with his statement because he told Skinner he would be there for 24 hours and then he would be gone. Skinner and Jennifer went back to the Gulf Terrace.

John took the first watch until 1 A.M. I walked down to Club Destin where Jean had called to make reservations for Captain Nick Sadler. A good name, one I always use when I'm in disguise. I told the desk clerk to give me a call around 12:30 A.M. due to an early hour business obligation.

When I relieved John at 1 A.M., he said they had prepared for bed, cut off the lights; however, the lights in one bedroom kept coming on every few minutes. This occurred for about an hour then finally it stopped. John said he guessed they had finally gone to sleep. After a while, I decided I would get out and walk around. Naturally I walked around building 20 just in case there was something I needed to see. There was very little to be heard or seen at 3:30 A.M., except for the soothing sound of surf. Too much sound, it almost put me to sleep as I stood there.

Finally I was able to shake my sleepiness and decided to go back to the car. About that time I saw a light go on in unit 2005. I could see the silhouettes of people moving around. I got real brave; went up the steps to the second floor hoping to get close enough to hear what they were saying to each other. It was 5 A.M. and they were having an argument. About the only thing I could make out was Jennifer telling Skinner that she had told him last night, those days were over. That his controlling her life had ended and he had better accept it now. That it would never change, not today and in fact, in his lifetime. They faded out as if they moved to another room. The dead bolt lock on one of the doors turned, meaning it was time for me to get to the ground level quickly. I almost didn't touch the steps as I sailed down the stairs. Once I was back inside the car, I saw Jennifer and Skinner going to their car. They drove off and I followed them at a great distance behind but there was really no need to follow. They went straight to the airport, got their plane and flew off into the dark skies.

I went back to the room and woke John. We both took our disguises off, took a shower, shaved and got ready for breakfast. Now it was time for us to make our pitch to start our plan into action. We called Lt. Black at his home, told him what we knew about the exchange at the dock and also what we thought would be coming off today. He told us he would call Sheriff Howard of Okaloosa County, Florida and that he would be in touch with us as soon as possible. He also asked us to give him 30 minutes, and to call him back, then he would tell us what to do.

I called him again when we finished eating. He told me Sheriff Howard was en route to our room at this very minute, and he should be there within 15 minutes. We paid our bill and walked back to our room. We were there only a few minutes before Sheriff Howard and three of his deputies arrived. We told them everything we knew that happened at the docks last night and what we thought might be happening today. With what we told him, the sheriff put a plan together that may enable him to catch more than just the pick up man.

When we got to the docks, the captain was moving around on the deck of the boat. We were pretty sure our man had not shown up. After two hours of waiting, two men drove up to the dock area, backed their truck to the <u>Dolphin Queen</u> and loaded five big ice chests on the back of their truck. One of the men went inside the boat with the captain for just a minute (must have been to give him the rest of the money). As the truck pulled on Highway 98 heading west toward Fort Walton, undercover deputies looking like men and women going to work were trailing the vehicle. The sheriff must have had at least six or seven cars with deputies from Destin to Fort Walton. They were passing the truck, passing one another, but there was one car that trailed along behind the truck never leaving its position and never allowing another vehicle to come between them and the truck. This continued on route 98 through Fort Walton.

After leaving Fort Walton, they turned into the driveway of a huge house with a large brick column fence. A search warrant was there within minutes. The deputies completely surrounded the house, then using force they entered the house, making their arrest and confiscating 20 big fish and 200 pounds of cocaine. They had already grabbed the captain and his crew. Sheriff Howard, his deputies and his office are to be praised for the efficiency in which his department handled the bust with such short notice.

The sheriff had assured us that we would not be mentioned in any way. Lt. Black had filled him in on what we were trying to do with this cocaine organization. The sheriff said he would keep it as quiet as possible as long as he could. That may give us enough time to trap Skinner and the other big wigs.

CHAPTER TWENTY-SEVEN
SATURDAY, DECEMBER 31, 1988

By the time we returned to Atlanta it was mid-afternoon. Knowing there would be messages on the office answering machine, we stopped to review them. Just as we anticipated there were several calls waiting for me. Jennifer had called three times wanting me to call her but mainly she wanted to know where I was at the present time. On the last of the three calls she sounded a little panicky. Lt. Day had called but that was not important to me. Jason had called three times and they were important. Something had happened in Texas.

Jason called early this morning according to the machine and he had sounded as if he was scared to death. His voice was excited and nervous sounding. I could hardly understand what he was trying to say. From what we gathered, there is something bad wrong in Houston. His explanation of what had happened went something like this. Four or five men had come to the cabin about daylight this morning. They called for them to come out with their hands up, telling them they were the Texas Rangers. Mark had told them we would as soon as we got dressed. When Mark opened the door and stepped outside, they opened fire on him. Mark was hit maybe twice but he was able to get back inside and close the door. They were showering the cabin with gunshots. One of the shots caught Martha in the head. It killed her instantly. Mark was firing at them but we didn't have a chance. I crawled to the trap door in the floor and escaped through the underground tunnel. He explained that the tunnel was about 50 feet long and came out close to a creek. He ran down the tunnel and to the creek to escape. Jason further agonized that Mark was to follow him but shots could still be heard when he cleared the tunnel and was running up the creek. He was sure they found the hidden trap door when the shooting stopped. "Mr. Grey, I am hurting for many reasons, but I'm also scared beyond belief." Jason related, "I know I'm the one they are pursuing and when they find me they will kill me," he added. Jason's last call was an hour before we had returned to the office.

Jean had called about 45 minutes ago wanting me to return her call. I wrote John a note telling him I was sorry about Mark. Also I was going to the corner drug store to make these calls. I gave him a code to get the right number for Jason to call and instructed him not to talk with Jason long enough for the call to be traced. The code for the phone number was simple, just add three numbers to each digit. I asked him to tell Jason to hang up and waste no time calling me.

When I got to the street, I noticed there were two of Atlanta's finest plainclothesmen trailing me. I went in to the drug store and called Lt. Black. When he answered I told him to get that weight off of me. I didn't need it. Within minutes a car came by, picking up the cops and drove off.

My calling was in progress. John had the pay phone number in code 569-6531. the real number being 892-9864. I hung up asking the owner to let me have the "Out of Order" sign to put on the door of the phone booth. The owner of the store was also my pharmacist and a good friend of mine. Her name was Melanie Sharpe. The name fit her to a tee for she was a real sharp lady in every respect. I also asked her if I could use her cell phone. She handed it to me and said,

"Help yourself." While waiting for Jason's call, I called Jennifer, but I couldn't seem to locate her. Jean was the next call on the list. She told me Jennifer had called her at home earlier this afternoon trying to locate me. She said Jennifer sounded as if she was in some kind of trouble and that she needed to talk to me. She also related that it sounded as if it could have been a matter of life and death. "Please be careful, Colby" was her last words before she hung up.

Finally after being there for about 20 minutes, the pay phone rang. It was Jason. He told me where he was now and how he was moving from one place to another to stay as safe as possible. He wanted to know what he was supposed to do, where was he to go and how could he get in touch with me. I told him he was doing a good job, to keep moving but make sure he moved where people wouldn't be able to recognize him. I told him to move with the crowd. Crowds would enable him to blend in. I also cautioned him to disguise himself, as that might help keep him alive. Hopefully Jason Myland won't be visible to anyone. I gave him John's cell phone number and let him know John would be on his way to Houston as soon as possible; hoping this would calm him down. I also told him there would be no need in calling John for at least four hours. That will give John time to get to Houston. I hung up feeling better about Jason.

After my conversation with Jason, I decided to call Jennifer again, this time on the pay phone. The only thing I heard from all of her phones was "Please leave a message." I left a message that I would be at the office in 10 minutes and to give me a call. I called Lt. Black, hoping to catch him at his desk but that was to no avail. They informed me that Lt.

Black would not be in until late afternoon. He and Lt. Day were together for the day, making busts. Lt. Black had told me they had picked up people going to the tobacco shops for cocaine here in Atlanta as well as other cities in Georgia and Alabama. The plan was well in motion and I had to find Jennifer and Skinner.

Upon returning to the office, John informed me Jennifer had just called leaving her home phone number for me to return her call. Grabbing the phone and quickly dialing her number but listening to the ring until she answered seemed like hours rather than seconds. Then there was that beautiful voice saying, "Hello, this is Jennifer." "This is Colby," I said, "Oh, thank God, I finally got you. Gilbert is out to kill you, he blames you for everything that has happened. After you called and left the message you were at your office he and three of his men left here on their way to your office to kill you," Jennifer stated. Jennifer was crying and asking me to please get out of the office. She then asked me to, "Please, let's leave and just get out of this place." She was in a state of panic. My answer was, "Sure, but it will take a few minutes."

After hanging up the phone, I told John what had happened. He began preparation for inviting Skinner and his goons into the office. He locked the outer office door. The door leading to my private office would be closed for our advantage. We took the tabletop from the outer office and situated it in front of my desk for more protection. It's a Plexiglas top about a half-inch thick. John got behind my desk with me, waiting for something to occur. We didn't have to wait long for Skinner's thugs to show up. We heard the outer office door rattle then the glass breaking. We were ready for them to enter the office. We had left the lights on in the outer office giving us a bird's eye view of what they were doing. We could see through the glass but they couldn't see in my office without opening the door. When they opened the door, we could see all four of them. Before they could cut on the lights, we had started the fireworks. The sound of gunfire rang throughout the office building. When the smoke had cleared, John and I had taken three of Skinner's men out while the fourth was lying wounded in the corner of the front office. I had emptied Sara plus my .32 special had been fired four times before the shooting stopped. Of course, Skinner was not with them and if he had been here, he was downstairs by now. I told John to wait for the police to get there and after he gave them all the details of the shooting; then hop on the plane to Houston to get Jason. I told him to take the first flight out of here and to be sure to take his cell phone with him. I left the office in a hurry, I ran down the stairs to the first floor, then to the street looking for Skinner. There he was waiting for his hired hands but he saw me about the same time I spotted him. When he saw me, he took off like a bat out of hell. That will give him a head start; in fact, he will have several minutes on me. My car was parked around back in the parking lot. I ran hard to my car, but Skinner had at least four to five minutes start on me by this time. I was on the street headed for Jennifer's house, driving like a maniac trying every short cut possible and I still didn't catch him. I closed the time gap between us, because I got there in time to see Skinner running toward the front door of Jennifer's house. I entered the long driveway to Jennifer's front door, stopping my car behind Skinner's. At the same time, the butler came running out the front door. He didn't' see me as he ran behind Skinner's car and when I placed a hand on his shoulder, he almost had a heart attack. He turned and looked at me with eyes full of fear. Then he said, "Mr. Skinner has gone crazy. He has Miss Jennifer by the neck waving a gun back and forth while yelling he's going to kill her, himself, and everybody." I told him to calm down and tell me how I could get in the house besides going through the front or back doors. He told me there was a door to the basement in the back of the house. I asked him to tell me where Skinner was located when he had left the house. He was scared out of his wits, all he could keep saying was that Mr. Skinner had gone completely crazy, and that he had Miss Jennifer around the neck dragging her up the stairs.

I ran around to the back of the house but stopped to reload both my weapons before entering the house. I was able to enter through the basement door. Going in the basement and up the basement steps to the kitchen was easy enough. I noted that the kitchen was clear, giving me a chance to ease toward the doorway going into the foyer. The foyer was a huge area with stairs on the right side leading to the second floor. I couldn't see anything from where I was standing. I stood under the second floor bedroom area. I still couldn't see anything. There was a huge mirror on the entire wall across from the steps leading upstairs. I was able to move around where I could see the upstairs level. That's when I saw Skinner waiting for me to appear. I heard Jennifer scream telling Skinner not to kill me. There she was getting up off the floor screaming at Skinner. That was my chance to run in a zigzag motion to a column about 20 feet away from me. When I got to the column I would be facing Skinner. Two shots rang out, the first shot came close but I don't know where the second shot went. Then I saw Jennifer wrestling with Skinner after I made it to the column. Before I had a clear shot, Skinner had subdued

Jennifer and was dragging her into one of the rooms. When the door closed, I moved very slowly, very cautiously to the stairs. Going up the steps as light-footed as I could, I moved toward the room they had entered moments before.

I heard Jennifer pleading with Skinner to stop this stupid killing. She would do whatever he wanted her to do if he would stop. They would go to another country or whatever he wanted, just please stop this killing, Jennifer continued. That didn't set too well with Skinner because he wanted me. I was the total blame for everything that had happened to him. He was cursing me now so I figured that this was a good time to get his attention. Yelling out to him I said, "Let Jennifer go. This is between you and me. We can settle this man to man or any other way you want to." He would have no part of my deal. His reply to me was, "Come on Pretty Boy. I want you to show me that pretty face just one more time." With those remarks, I kicked the door open and jumped to the side, which was out of his firing range according to where his voice was coming from. Skinner's gun went off two more times. That is exactly what I wanted him to do. That meant he had fired shots three and four leaving him two more shots. There was a small table in the hallway. I picked it up and threw it into the room causing Skinner to fire without knowing he was firing at a table. That left one shot in his chamber, if my counting was correct.

I knew I shouldn't do this but I did it anyway. I dove into the room hoping for him to miss with his last shot. Brave? No not hardly, I was just trying to save Jennifer and get Skinner. Skinner's pistol rang out twice; the last shot got me in the leg. I had not contemplated a second gun nor figured he carried a reload on his person. When the second shot caught my leg, Sara went sailing across the room about six feet from where I was lying. Skinner began to laugh. He knew the upper hand was all his now. He turned Jennifer loose and started to move toward me, which was his mistake. Jennifer picked up a vase, hit him in the head stunning him for a moment. Jennifer began to run toward me. This was her mistake. Skinner shot her in the back twice before I could clear my .32 from the holster. I emptied all five shots into Skinner's chest and stomach. I then crawled toward Jennifer begging her to, "Hold on, hold on." She said to me as I reached her side, "Colby, don't leave me. I'm afraid of dying." I replied, "I won't leave you, darling." Her reply was a smile and then weakly she said, "I love you Colby Grey." I told her I loved her too. She pointed to her desk and said, "Letter for you." Her last words were, "I love you, please forgive me." These words came with her last gasp of air and then her eyes rolled back. I knew Jennifer was dead. Tears began flowing down my face like someone had opened the floodgates to my heart. Love had been mine twice in my life and both loves met with a violent death. Two beautiful lives snuffed out by a crazy individual with a gun trying to kill me. I crawled to the desk, found the letter addressed to me, put it in my coat pocket and crawled back to Jennifer.

The butler must have called the police and the emergency squad. I could hear sirens off in a distance, getting closer and closer until they were in front of Jennifer's house. Tears still ran down my face as I sat next to Jennifer waiting for someone to come over and check her, or someone to at least find out what had happened. The cops and paramedics were everywhere when Lt. Black walked in with Lt. Day. I had left both Sara and the special lying on the floor. When the medics had me ready to go to the hospital, Lt. Black came over and asked me if I felt like telling him how it all happened. After telling him what had happened in detail, I said, the .357 magnum and the .32 special are mine. I would appreciate you taking care of them for me." Lt. Black assured me that he would see to it, that I would get both of them back after the investigation.

On the way to the hospital, I thought about Lt. Day smiling and talking, not suspecting a thing. When we locate Skinner's books, he won't be smiling so much. That's the only reason he's not in jail at the present, is because we don't have Skinner's books yet. Those books will prove beyond a doubt that Day is a dirty cop. It's just a matter of time before we nail him and be able to close this huge cocaine case. I also thought about John and Jason. I wondered if they were safe. I will call them as soon as possible to find out what has happened on their end of the plot. My thoughts kept going back to Jennifer and about the letter I have in my pocket. The feelings I had for her and the love she had for me was real. I knew that feeling had to be true. She proved she loved me by giving her life to save mine. We finally arrived at the hospital and as they were rolling me to the emergency room, I thought how much I had loved Jennifer. The last thing I remember hearing was the doctor saying that the bone in my leg was splintered from the bullet and that he would have to put me to sleep in order to set it properly.

CHAPTER TWENTY-EIGHT
SATURDAY, DECEMBER 31,1988

I woke up in the hospital with Lt. Black standing over me. My leg was in a cast and hurting tremendously. My stomach felt like I had not eaten in a week, even though it had only been about 24 or so hours. Lt. Black was smiling while he was telling me I was going to be all right. I will be laid up for a few days but other than that, I would be fine. Then the nurse came in with some food for me. Even though it was hospital food I ate all of it and enjoyed it. After finishing my meal, I asked Lt. Black if he had found Skinner's books. He replied that he had not. Also I inquired about John but he had not called Lt. Black. I needed my pants to get my wallet and when Lt. Black handed them to me I realized my wallet was not there. I called the nurse and she informed me that according to hospital policy, all valuables were locked away but that she would promptly locate them and bring them to me.

John was the first person I called. When he answered he said, "Where have you been? I've been calling you at home and the office ever since I left to come to Houston." He continued, "If you had not called today, I was coming back to Atlanta, you were beginning to worry me." I told him what had happened on my end, where I was, how bad it was, and why they had decided to keep me in the hospital. "Now tell me about Jason and what has happened." He began by telling me Jason was all right and standing beside him at the moment. Then I told him to stay there for a few days at least until I was out of the hospital. We concluded our conversation and hung up. Lt. Black was about to leave.

He said he would see me tomorrow and I told him thanks. With a high sign, he left.

The nurse handed me my coat so I could find the envelope Jennifer had left me. It had **COLBY** in big bold letters. I though how much I had missed Jennifer during the holidays but now I would never be able to see her again. I won't even be able to go to her funeral planned for 2 P.M. January 2. I opened the envelope. It contained a letter addressed to me and also there was a key that looked like a safe deposit box key. As I opened the letter tears again appeared in my eyes because deep inside me I knew this was it, there would be nothing else from Jennifer. I began to read the letter from Jennifer.

Dearest Colby:

If you are reading this letter, then I am no longer around because Gilbert told me he would kill me before he would give me up to you. My only hope is that you are able to read this because no one knew Gilbert Skinner the way I did. No one knew what he was capable of doing; he is an evil man.

I want you to know just how much I loved you. I never thought I would ever love anyone with so much passion, but then you came into my life. The first time we met and talked, I knew there was a strong attraction for both of us. I could see it in your eyes and feel it inside me. There was a passion there that would eventually pull us together. You were too much of a gentleman to make the first move so I had to come to you. I loved you that much because of the kind of man you were.

After we had made love for the first time, I knew we were meant to be together. There was something special between us, very special. I had never known love before you. I had experienced sex in my life, but never before had I experienced love until you.

My love for you is real, Colby. I know it was real love from the very beginning or at least it was real on my part. My darling, always remember me as the Jennifer you knew. Not the Jennifer, you will read about in my diary. You treated me with respect for the woman you met, the woman you came to know. There was no other reason for that respect except you liked me, the woman. Most men were always seeking other things from me, but you made me proud to be a woman.

So in years to come, remember, *I LOVED YOU WITH ALL MY HEART. Jennifer*

P.S. Colby, the key is to my safe deposit box. I have made some arrangements and I would like for you to take care of them for me. Remember when you read my diary, please don't hate me. Just remember I had never experienced real love before you. J.M.

After reading the letter, I tried to concentrate on the bowl games that were being played today. It was difficult! I even tried to get hopes up of the possibility of going home tomorrow. Jean came to see me and brought some of her wonderful goodies. As I eat these cookies, which were my favorite - peanut butter, I continued to watch the game.

John called about 7 P.M. wanting to know if Lt. Black had been able to arrest Lt. Day. I related that the books had not been located as of yet and this made it difficult for Lt.

Black to make anything stick on Day. It would be just a matter of time before we find the books, then bingo; it would be over. We could make all the arrests in the Atlanta area that had not already been made. I think we have gotten everyone at the tobacco company that was involved. That seemed to please John, then I said, "Come what may, this case is almost over." John's comment was "You are so right, Colby. It came, it went and we solved." With that statement, we hung up the phone.

CHAPTER TWENTY-NINE
SUNDAY, JANUARY 1, 1989

This day has been a long, hard day. What a New Year's. Trying to learn to walk with crutches was quite difficult. Anyway it's over and I didn't see much of any game. I am about to go to sleep with the help of a sleeping pill. Maybe sleep will help ease my pain over Jennifer's death and my constant thinking about the case.

CHAPTER THIRTY
MONDAY, JANUARY 2, 1989

This was one of the hardest days of my life. Jennifer was buried today. The doctor had told me it was best not to leave the hospital just yet. It was tough not being able to go to her funeral Jean went and came by to tell me about the service.

When she left, I fell asleep and slept until the nurses woke me to give me a sleeping pill. I won't ever understand why they wake a patient to give them a sleeping pill. Oh, well, that's medicine for you. I guess.

CHAPTER THIRTY-ONE
TUESDAY, JANUARY 3, 1989

Another dull day in the hospital but the doctor did say I could go home tomorrow for sure!!

CHAPTER THIRTY-TWO
WEDNESDAY, JANUARY 4, 1989

The doctor came in this morning with a smile on his face and said, "Colby, you may go home today." Jean was the person I called to see if she would mind coming to pick me up. Of course she didn't mind, and she said she would be here within the hour. She arrived 45 minutes later, even before they could get my discharge papers in order. However, it was not long before they rolled me down the hall to the entrance where she was waiting with the car. As I transferred from the chair to the car, using my crutches, I realized how sore my armpits were because of all the therapy I had been through the last couple of days. My cast was only to my knee, making it a little easier for me to use the crutches. The doctor had also given me good news saying he may put a walking cast on before too many more days. Of course, he added, it was according to how I progressed at home. With that in mind, I vowed to work really hard, hoping I could soon put down the crutches and walk on my own.

Jean had already erased all the messages that had accumulated on the answering machine. She's always trying to look after my feelings as well as my well being. She brought me some coffee and a donut. The first order of work was to get Lt. Black on the phone, which she did. I told Lt. Black I would like to rid my office of all the bugs that had been planted there earlier in the case. He assured me he would be in route shortly to rid me of my problems. After hanging up, I asked Jean when she got the office cleaned up, "A couple of days ago," she replied.

Lt. Black got to my office sooner than I expected bringing with him a bug detector. He did a good job finding all of them. There were bugs everywhere, in the lamps, under the tables, in the phones, in the lights, in the light switches and even under the coffeepot. When Lt. Black was sure he had found and collected all the devices for evidence he told me some of them were department issued bugs. After putting his equipment away, we talked about Skinner's books. We knew he had kept books because Jason had told me about them in Mexico. He had told me Skinner was very particular about everything, especially his books. His books are somewhere in his suite of offices in the Building of Glass.

Lt. Black waited for me to call John before he left for the Building of Glass. When I got John on the phone, I told him to bring Jason back to Atlanta and to be sure they wore their disguises because we didn't want anyone knowing Jason was back in Atlanta. John said, "Good, we will be on the next flight." I told John we had a lot of things to take care of upon his arrival and just make sure he kept Jason under wraps. John's reply was as always, "Will do," as we hung up. Lt. Black was walking out the door, when I told him I would see him later.

I worked in the office for a couple of hours on paper work that had to be done before other things could be taken care of. The expenses were the main issue; how much we had been paid on expenses by Jennifer and how much we spent on plane fares, motels, rental cars, gas and food. It was all mounting up. Jennifer had been very generous with payment.

When I finished all the paper work that I could do, I decided it was time to go home. I had gotten very tired staying up this long. There was one more thing I needed to take care of before I left. There was the need to talk to Joan Harrison, but I had no way of getting in touch with her. Lt. Black had already told me she always called him. Calling the airport asking to speak with the flight attendant supervisor was my next move. Holding the phone for a few minutes didn't really bother me at all!! This was important, besides there was nothing else to do at the present. Then a voice came over the phone saying, "This is Tammy Dentson, may I help you?" I wanted to know if she was the supervisor who helped me the other day. I gave her the particulars telling her my name and the situation. Ms. Dentson told me I needed to speak with Melinda Harper, the head of personnel. She then transferred me to Melinda's office. There was a pause; then the answer came, "Ms. Harper's office, this is her secretary Elizabeth, may I help you?" Here I go again, with the same old routine, explaining everything again. Elizabeth told me to hold a moment. The next voice I heard was Melinda Harper. Ms. Harper said, "Mr. Grey, what can I do for you?" I explained my dilemma, and told her all I wanted her to do was call Joan informing her I needed to speak with her as soon as possible. Ms. Harper said she would take care of it for me. Telling her thanks was easy.

The phone rang again about 15 minutes later. It was Joan. She related that she was doing fine and was enjoying her time with her son and family. I told her what was going on in Atlanta, and it didn't surprise her at all. She said she had read all about it in the local paper and that she had been extremely worried about me. Then, I lowered the heavy news that Jason had been found; and he was alive and well. There was a long silence before she said anything, the only sound was sobbing as if she was trying not to cry. I also told her that I had not told him about her or her son. I replied, "I really haven't had a chance to speak with him yet; however, I will. Do you want me to tell him about his son or do you want to do it? I will not tell him without your permission." Her reply was, "That is a nice gesture, and I understand why Jennifer thought you were so special." She then said I should do what I though best because she trusted me completely. "Thanks," I replied. Joan also shared the thought that she was proud Jason was alive and that it won't be hard telling his son about his father. Then I told her, she could return to work in a couple of days. Joan was very glad to get that piece of information. As we finished our conversation, she said, "Colby, on second thought, let me tell Jason about me and our son." I said, "That's very good to hear."

Now everything is taken care of and the rest seemed much closer than it did earlier. "Home, here I come!" I asked Jean to call me a cab because I needed to go home and rest. She said, "Nonsense, I will take you home and see that you are settled before I leave." That will be wonderful I thought.

CHAPTER THIRTY-THREE
TUESDAY, JANUARY 5,1989

Rest is the very best medicine for a weary soul. Sleeping 10 full hours makes you feel a little tight in the morning. Only after having a good hot shower does the tightness begin to loosen and the muscles relax. I had to put a trash bag over my cast to keep it from getting wet. It took me longer to get ready than it would have normally. That is to be expected with this weight on my leg. When I finally got ready and was about to phone a taxi, there was someone ringing my doorbell. It was Jean, of course, asking if I needed a ride to the office. I just smiled at her and said, "Yes, thank you."

On our way to work, we talked about many things but mostly about Jennifer. Jean told me that she had been fooled badly by Jennifer. Her feeling for you had to be real, not only real but everlasting. This conversation made me feel good, just knowing someone else saw what I had seen in Jennifer. I told Jean how much I appreciated her and what she had just said about Jennifer. It really meant a great deal to me.

When we got to the office, John had already called telling me to give him a call at his apartment. I did after I got settled at my desk. The phone rang about four times before John answered. We talked about Jason and what we needed to do today but mostly about how I felt physically, mentally and emotionally. He knew how I really felt about Jennifer and how I must be hurting at this very moment. It's wonderful to have good friends who really care about you. John wanted to know what we were going to do about Jason. I told him to leave Jason at his apartment today and to tell him to keep the door locked and not to answer the phone or the door. I also told John not to let anyone know Jason was there.

Jean brought me a cup of coffee then went across the street to get some donuts. About the time she closed the door the phone rang. It was Joan Harrison telling me she wanted to come as soon as possible to talk with Jason. I told her that would be fine. I asked for her phone number so that I could call her as soon as I thought it was safe for both of them. She revealed that she would have to call me because where they were staying there was no phone service. That seemed strange. Are there still motels that don't carry phone service for their guests? I told her to call me again tomorrow.

Jean came in with a box of donuts; I ate two in a hurry with another cup of coffee. By the time I had gotten a third donut with still another cup of coffee, John walked in smiling. He gave Jean the high sign and then looked at me and said, "I sure am proud to see you, especially in one piece." Then he wanted to know every detail about my encounter with Skinner. After going over every detail in the order it occurred, John told me I was one lucky man. He also stated that he owed me an apology because I was right about Jennifer, that he was wrong, "Sorry, boss." "Thank you, John" I answered! John informed me about Jason, how frightened he was but he did a good job staying calm. He didn't see any sign of trouble while he was with Jason.

The case was close to being solved but we still had not found Tracy Love or what his connection is in the cocaine ring. Maybe we will have that answer when Lt. Black finds Skinner's books.

A visit to Jennifer's banks was the top priority today. I need to speak with the bank president, even though I have the key to Jennifer's safe deposit box. That doesn't mean I can just open it because my signature was not on file. Because of this, there will probably need to be a court order. Signatures are very important where safe deposit boxes are concerned. If a court order is needed, one will be obtained. We will know once we talk with the president or bank manager.

The president of the bank was a very nice individual. He knew who I was because Jennifer had taken care of everything two days prior to her death. She had given him a signed affidavit telling the bank if anything happened to her that Colby Grey would be her power of attorney. The paper had been notarized making it legal. She definitely had a premonition of what was going to take place. Maybe she knew Skinner only too well. Perhaps he told her he was going to kill her as well as me. Whatever the reason, she had done her job well. The president took us down to the area where the safe deposit boxes were located. He took care of everything; the only thing I had to do was sign a couple of bank forms.

The president took my key to the bank official in charge of the safe deposit area. With the bank's key and my key, he was able to open the door to a huge safe deposit box. A private room was provided for me to go through Jennifer's belongings. When they brought me the box, I called out to John to go buy us a briefcase plus a small piece of luggage to hold the contents of the box. I then proceeded to go through the box to see what Jennifer had deemed important in her life. There it was - a ledger book. Could it be Skinner's book? Holding my breath I prayed that this is the book. I slowly opened it. It was the ledger with all his transactions of dealing with the cocaine trafficking. There was Tracy Love's name but Skinner had spelled it Traci. The letter I instead of Y prompted me to wonder if we had been looking for a male all this time when in reality Traci was a female. As I closed the record book and looked farther in the box, I could see envelopes with rubber bands around them. As I took the rubber band off, I counted five different envelopes with rubber bands around them. As I took the rubber band off, I counted 15 different envelopes with one being very thick. There were also four boxes about the size of shoeboxes or maybe a little larger. I took the box that had the number one on it and opened it first. Inside I found a note from Jennifer lying on a stack of hundred dollar bills. The note told me that this was clean money. This money was part of what she inherited from her parents along with her part of the business. This money had been in CD's for years until recently when she surrendered them for cash. She had told me there was over a half-million dollars in these four boxes in hundred dollar bills. The note continued telling me she wanted this to be mine. "Consider it payment for what you have done for me or for solving the case that freed me from Skinner," she wrote. She indicated I would understand when I read her diary what she meant by that statement. Closing the boxes of money, I looked back to the safe deposit box. There was her diary on the bottom as if it was looking at me. I picked it up and decided not to open it until I could read the entire story of her life alone at home.

When John returned with the briefcase and luggage, we filled them up with all of Jennifer's private belongings and money. John carried the briefcase and pulled the luggage. I struggled hard to keep up with him because of the crutches. My armpits were really sore, since I used the crutches so much yesterday. Saying thanks to the bank president and manager, we were on our way to the office.

John knew Skinner's book was in the briefcase because I had pointed it out to him. As soon as we got to the office, I told Jean to call Lt. Black and tell him what we had found. See if he wants to come over immediately. John was examining the book very carefully when all of a sudden his eyes lit up like candles. He said, "Colby, did you see, of course you saw, Traci Love's name spelled with an "I" not a "Y"? I smiled and told him it had never occurred to either of us that Traci could be female. When John had finished going through Skinner's records he smiled with that smirk grin of his and said, "We've got that son-of-a-bitch now." He was referring to Lt. Day because his name was in the records several times where he had taken dirty money. There was one name that was not logged in the cocaine ledger. Jennifer's name was no where to be found. (I was thankful for that.)

Lt. Black made good time getting to the office. He was excited as he walked in telling John to let him see what we had in writing. Handing the ledger to Lt. Black, John excused himself to get another cup of coffee. Lt. Black looked at me with his unique smile, then he said, "Colby, now I can put the clamps on Day, this is great evidence." Lt. Black also wanted to know if this was all the evidence Jennifer had in her safe deposit box. Before I could answer, John entered the room telling him we hadn't finished going through it yet but we would let him know as soon as possible. John smiled and said, "You will be the first to know." Lt. Black continued smiling as he took the ledger and left. He was on his way to see the captain, the judge, or anyone else he needed to see to get a warrant for Day's arrest. He wanted everything to be legal when he made the arrest. Lt. Black's thoughts had to be on ridding the department of one more dirty cop.

The envelopes she left me were full of things for me to do. The first envelope was filled with papers from her lawyer with instructions on how to make everything I do legal. Jennifer had taken care of this. I had power of attorney and there were papers that notarized me as the legal person of her affairs. These papers were signed by Jennifer and her attorney. There was a list of things she wanted me to do in the envelope. The first thing that was important to her, was taking care of her servants. She had all their names with what each one should receive listed; she had done such a good job organizing and arranging her affairs, I could easily take care of what she wanted.

It was awfully tough to go through her material, reading what she had prepared for me to do. It reminded me that another piece of my heart was gone because of love. Love sucks, twice I have been in love, and twice I had lost it. Not only did I lose the girls, but also they lost their lives because of me. There won't be another love for Colby Grey.

As I read on, Jennifer had her attorney to assist me in every way possible in order to carry out her wishes. He had access to all her money except the cash she had left for me. The next envelope was filled with evidence Lt. Black would want or need. There were three tapes in this envelope as well as signed documents by different individuals receiving money. There was also a note from Traci Love in this envelope that simply stated that she would be in Atlanta Thursday and she expected to have lunch with Gilbert. (She expected to have lunch with? That sounded like an order, not a request) This made me wonder if Skinner was not the top man in this cocaine ring. Maybe we were not at the close of the case yet. There may be more ends that need to be tied together before we solve it completely.

We spent several hours going through the envelopes, checking out the different receipts. We only stopped long enough to eat lunch that Jean had called in. I was beginning to get tired when the phone rang. It was Lt. Black informing me that he was coming over to bring Sara and my .32 special. He also related that the arrest papers were being written as we speak and almost in the same breath wanted to know if we had found anything else that might help with the arrest. My answer was, "I think so Lt." He was pleased with the answer and added that he was anxious to get there to pick up the evidence on Rodney Day. "I'll see you in a few minutes," were his last words before hanging up the phone.

John left going to his apartment to check on Jason and also to take him some dinner in the event we worked late. I doubt that I will be working late because this body of mine needs rest and more rest. As I related this to Jean she let me know right quick that she thought this was a splendid idea. I told her that I wanted to wait for Lt. Black and John to arrive before I departed.

My decision, about what to do with the money Jennifer had left for me, was not made at this moment. The four boxes of hundred dollar bills were put in my safe at the office. Of course, I had not said anything to John or Jean about the money. Whatever decision I reach, they will know and get their share, because they are more than just Associates, they are family. The decision has to be made by me and me alone. With that in mind, I will keep it under wraps until later.

Lt. Black walked in with that smile on his face and asked, "Where is it Colby?" I immediately handed him three receipts that Rodney Day had signed for an amount of $75,000. Each receipt was for $25,000. All Lt. Black could say was, "OH YES, OH YES! This is great evidence." I then explained to him that there were three tapes I had not had a chance to review, as soon as they were reviewed he would be informed as to what was on them.

Lt. Black turned and stopped saying, "I almost forgot why I called you in the first place. Here is Sara and your .32 special." As he walked out the door he was singing "Oh, Happy Days." Jean came in laughing and saying that the Lt. is certainly a happy man these days. "You are right. The evidence he got today would make any honest cop happy," I commented.

Again Jean knew what my thoughts were because she brought my pistol cleaning outfit in for me. She knew I would want to clean my weapons as soon as possible. Cleaning a weapon after they have been fired is important because you never know when you will need to use them. I stopped what I was doing with Jennifer's material and cleaned Sara, then my .32 special. As I was finishing wiping down the special, John came in to report that everything was fine with Jason.

Jean had stopped John for a few moments before he entered my office. I know she must have been telling him to take me home so I could get some much-needed rest, because John's first comment was "Colby, looks like it's about time to call it a day." Grabbing the three tapes, Jennifer's diary and my weapons, I was ready to go. I am too tired to review the tapes tonight, but I will have them with me anyway.

As soon as I got to the apartment, I brushed my teeth and combed my hair and then proceeded to the important agenda. I got myself a glass of milk, a banana and a moon pie. Some menu! But it is one of my favorites. Afterward, I brushed my teeth again and was ready for bed. Today had been an extra long one and it was only 4 P.M.

CHAPTER THIRTY-FOUR
FRIDAY, JANUARY 6, 1989

Waking up a 2:30 A.M. is not good, but I had slept about
10 hours and was ready to get up. I ate some cereal with a
banana, took a shower and shaved; all of which made me
feel like a new person. Now I was ready to do the work I
had been putting off since getting out of the hospital.
Listening to the tapes was the first thing on the agenda.
Jennifer had numbered them one, two and three in the order
she wished them to be heard.

Slipping the tape numbered one into the tape recorder,
turning the volume up and settling back on the sofa, I began
to listen to some real evidence. Skinner had gone through
their operations of the cocaine ring step by step. It was just
like we had figured it out. The only difference I found was
that the ring was much larger than we had anticipated. In
tape number one no names were mentioned at all, only how
the cocaine was handled during shipment and what was
done to it before it went on the streets. The distribution
process was a smooth machine, working all over the
southeastern states.

In tape number two, finances were discussed. The gross
amount coming in monthly was astounding. The amount of
half a million dollars was collected monthly in the
beginning and had grown to the staggering amount of three
to five million monthly recently. There were names on this
tape that were common with Jason's list of names. Traci
Love's name was mentioned at the end of this tape. Skinner
mentioned that Ms. Love's take was much too large. That
was it, no clue to her identity nor how he contacted her. The
location of Ms. Love is still a mystery. Rodney Day was a

paid cop. He was paid to help keep the cocaine moving smoothly in Atlanta. His payment was $25,000 quarterly. In other words, Day was paid $100,000 yearly to be a dirty cop. Money can make people do anything because it along with the love of it are evil.

Tape number three was about Jennifer's involvement with Skinner's cocaine ring. She had picked up Jason's smoking tobacco many times after they were married. She knew exactly what she was doing when she picked up the packages. Finally she had been informed that Jason was stealing money from the organization. Skinner had told Jennifer that Jason was suspected of stealing anywhere from a quarter to half a million dollars monthly. As Jennifer continued, I began to wonder if we had really solved the case as of today. Skinner had planned the murder but he wanted to get his money back before he eliminated Jason. He didn't get the money nor did he eliminate Jason. Skinner knew this because the man he sent to take care of Jason never returned. That was how Jennifer had known that Jason had not committed suicide. Incidentally, these were her exact comments on the tape.

I finished listening to the tapes about 5 A.M. I took a break and prepared another cup of coffee before reading Jennifer's diary. I knew once involved with the reading of her diary, I would completely forget and never take another drink of coffee. So I finished off the cup before I began reading.

The diary started a year before Skinner and her mother were married. There was nothing of importance in her first year, only a child writing her thoughts. She told how Gilbert Skinner had been good to her before the marriage to her mother. He had been just that good to her mother. Jennifer loved her mother very much and she grew to care a lot for Gilbert because of his attitude toward the two of them.

Saturday, 1963: (As with most children, if days were used many times the date didn't accompany it) Mother and Gilbert are getting married today. (Later that day.) The wedding was big and beautiful. There were a lot of people at our house to see them marry. I hope they will be happy.

Sunday: Mother and Gilbert came home from their honeymoon today. They went to Spain for two weeks. Mother seems to be very happy. She told me they had a wonderful time.

Saturday: Mother and Gilbert have been back for almost two weeks now and they seem to be happy but I did hear them arguing for the first time today.

Monday: I know why mother and Gilbert were arguing now. Gilbert had fired Linda, our maid that has been with us for years. He told Mother he would not live here if she stayed. I don't know why.

Wednesday: Gilbert brought Carrie home with him today and told us she was our new maid. She started working today but she didn't' seem to know a lot about what she was supposed to do.

Friday: It has been almost three weeks since Carrie became our maid. She is very nice; she likes doing things with me. Maybe it is because she is a lot younger than Linda. She is a very pretty lady and a lot of fun, but I still miss Linda.

Saturday: Mother and Gilbert have been gone for about a month now; they told me it was a business trip. I guess that's why I couldn't go.

Sunday: Carrie has gotten everything ready for me to go to my new school, a girl's academy. I am going into the sixth grade this year, because I was able to complete both the fourth and fifth grades last year.

Saturday: The first week here at the academy had been a lot of fun. I have made a lot of friends this week, girls that know a lot about life or at least they seem to. They are teaching me things I was not aware of; for example, all about sex.

Tuesday: Mother came with our chauffeur to take me home for the Christmas holidays. I was so glad to see Mother. I love her so much. I really have missed her while being here at school.

Wednesday: I went horseback riding today with Mother. We had a wonderful time but Mother didn't seem to be as happy as she was the last time I saw her.

Thursday: Mother and I went shopping for Christmas today. We bought many presents for the people we care about. I even bought one for Linda and also one for Carrie. Carrie has also become my friend. Mother felt better today.

Friday: I asked Carrie if she would go shopping with me today. She gladly accepted. She said we would have such a good time, and we did. We shopped for special gifts; my special gift was for Mother while Carrie was looking for something special for her boyfriend. She would not talk about him at all. I finally found what I wanted to get Mother at Holmans' Jewelry Store. It was a beautiful brooch that my mother did not have, so I bought it for her present. Carrie got her boyfriend a gold money clip and had his initials engraved on it. I had a good time with Carrie today. She's really a nice and pretty lady.

Sunday: Christmas Day is always a big day at our house because there are so many things to do. We always go to church, but we didn't go today. Gilbert made the announcement at the breakfast table that he would like to rest today because he was leaving for Europe on Tuesday. Mother jumped up from the table and asked why she wasn't informed about this before now. Carrie dropped a tray of eggs and Gilbert told Mother he didn't have to answer to anyone about what he planned or did. This did not start our Christmas Day off on the right foot. After lunch Mother got everyone around the Christmas tree, and I gave out the gifts. I think everyone liked their gifts, especially Mother. She just loved the brooch.

Tuesday: Gilbert left for Europe today. Mother seemed to be a little down, but she still wanted me to play the piano and sing for her. I asked Carrie to join us, but she said she was too tired. She wanted to get some rest.

Sunday: I love my mother, but I am so glad that I am going back to school. I really do miss my friends, something I had none of before coming to this school. Each one of us had something to tell about the holidays. The older girls in junior high grades were telling stories that were much more interesting than ours so we went over to their side of the room to listen. Their stores were about sex and whether they were true or not, they certainly were interesting to listen to.

(That was Jennifer's last entry in her diary for the school term)

Monday: I came home for a couple of days before returning to summer school. By going to summer school I can pass three years of schooling in one calendar year at the academy. Mother and I had a long talk about my being able to skip years the way I was trying to do. She assured me I was mature enough to handle it.

Tuesday: I enjoyed being with Mother because my love for her has grown so much. However I was ready to return to school to be with my friends.

Friday: Here it is Christmas holidays and I am an eighth grader. I am 11 years old but everyone says I look a lot older than I am. My body is beginning to develop and I had my first period last month. If I had not come to this school, I would have been scared to death. My friends tell me I am too young to start my monthly periods. That's okay because I am ready to be a teenager; I like these changes in my body. Terri, my best friend came home with me today. She will spend two nights with me before her mother comes to pick her up on Sunday.

Saturday: A big day for Terri and me. We had such a wonderful time all day long. We went horseback riding this morning, had lunch with Mom, and played games in the game room until 3 P.M., and then we went swimming in the lap pool until we were told it was time to get ready for dinner. At the dinner table, I asked Mother if we could go to a movie. Mother told us we could if we had enough money. Gilbert told me that he would give us the money and then he stood up, took out his money clip and gave me $20; I almost flipped. I could hardly tell him thanks. It was the clip Carrie bought for her boyfriend's Christmas gift.

Gilbert is Carrie's boyfriend, NO WAY! At the movie all I could think of was Mother, Gilbert and Carrie.

Monday: This was the last day I would spend with Mother before going back to school. During the visit, I noticed that Mother had started drinking a lot of wine, but I had not seen her drunk. After Mom and I agreed it was time for bed, I had a longing to slip out, climb the tree next to the guest house and dream as I often did before going away to school. Well maybe I had seen something earlier that caused me to want to play a little "I Spy." I saw Carrie enter the guest house earlier this afternoon and after dinner I noticed Gilbert boldly enter the guest house through the front door. What I saw happening in the bedroom between Gilbert and Carrie was all the education I had learned from the older girls only it was live action.

Tuesday: Mother and I talked about many things on our trip back to school. Finally I told her what I had seen the night before. She looked at me and began to cry. She told me that she knew what was going on in her own home, but she couldn't do anything about it. Then she said something totally unrelated. She said she only wanted me to study hard at school. That would make her happy.

(Jennifer must have had a hard time dealing with her mother's treatment by Skinner because she did not write in her diary for almost five years, the best I could tell. The next entry in the diary was after her mother had committed suicide)

March 20, 1970: Gilbert is guilty of murder because he killed my mother just as if he personally forced those pills down her throat. She lived with his carrying on with Carrie right under her nose in her own home. Gilbert Skinner, I will destroy you if it's the last thing I do. I will punish you for what you did to my mother. I hate you, Gilbert Skinner.

March 1971: I had a date with a Georgia Tech football player tonight, he may be the one I need. My plan to destroy Gilbert will be put into motion before long.

April 3, 1971: Johnny and I have been dating now for over a month. It finally happened. Johnny and I made love. It hurt me real bad and Johnny got scared because of all the blood. Johnny was awfully clumsy but he says he loves me. That does not matter to me because I'm using Johnny to get to Gilbert.

June 26, 1971: Johnny and I have been making love for a month now without using any kind of protection. I have missed one monthly period so I took a pregnancy test and guess what! I AM, IT WAS POSITIVE! This is the first part of my plan to destroy Gilbert. When it happens Gilbert, the whole world will know what kind of man you are now with all my mother's money.

July 4, 1971: A big party was held at my home today; anybody who is anybody was here. Gilbert was proud to show me off to all his friends. He's always telling me every time I come home, how pretty I have become since I'm growing up. Every time Gilbert wanted a drink tonight I would get it for him. I would make it stronger each time hoping he would soon become intoxicated. He steadily reaches the point of no return and when the last guest left, I had to help Gilbert up to my room. By the time I had gotten a shower, Gilbert was sound asleep. It was time to go to work on my plan. I had gotten a small amount of plasma from a friend of mine who was a nurse. I took some of the plasma and spread it on my pajamas. It was time to put my plan in motion so I crawled in the bed next to him. Gilbert was a lot smarter than I was because he began to move around in the bed. All of a sudden he was on top of me like a wild man. He tore off my pajamas while he was still on top of me. I fought him with every ounce of strength I had but he won the battle. It was painful and I began to cry and I continued to cry for a long time, all night long. This was the worst night of my life, a disaster - instead of trapping Gilbert, he trapped me. He has me right where he wants me. I hate Gilbert Skinner.

July 5, 1971: Gilbert told me today that if I was trying to involve him in a situation where there was a baby concerned, it was a lost cause because he had mumps when he was a boy. They had left him sterile. He said it was because the mumps had gone down on him as the old folks say. He was incapable of fathering a child. Gilbert has beaten me at my own game. It would not have worked anyway. "Damn you Gilbert Skinner, I hate you."

September 2, 1971: I went to New York to have an abortion at Gilbert's insistence. I changed my mind. I just couldn't go through with it because I would be murdering a human being. I couldn't stand the thoughts or taking a baby's life. Gilbert went into a rage; I had never seen him so mad. We argued for a while then he got out of control and slapped me across the face and pushed me backward over the sofa. I must have hit my head because I woke up in the hospital. They told me they were sorry about the loss of my baby. I had miscarried. I hate Gilbert Skinner. I have cried for the past three days. Gilbert told me if I ever tried to cross him again I would live to regret it because he would personally cut my face up so badly that no one would ever recognize me. I hate him with a passion. Maybe one day I will find a man who will be able to stand up to Gilbert. Then I will destroy him. I hate him so much.

June 1, 1979: We hired Jason Myland a few years back to head up our security. I knew he was a hard worker, also he was someone I thought I could trust. We started dating without anyone knowing about us. I thought Jason might be the man to stand up to Gilbert.

June 30, 1979: Jason and I have been dating for a month and we have decided to get married. I called Gilbert from Las Vegas to break the news to him. He went crazy over the phone, telling me he would have it annulled. He threatened us and told me to just wait; I had something coming from him. He reminded me that he had once told me never to cross him, and he reminded me of this again. He told me what an underhanded movement this was and he would certainly be getting back with us. I cut him off; told him he was nothing more than my stepfather and I would marry anyone I wanted to. I also reminded him that he no longer has anything to do with me. My last statement for him was to cool off and we would see him in a month.

July 4, 1979: Our honeymoon was in France. Jason and I planned how we were going to ruin Gilbert. If we were able to destroy him, everything would be ours.

(Jennifer also wrote something that touched my nerve a little. She had written how tender Jason was when they made love. Not like the animal passion that Gilbert always showed toward her body. Jennifer stated that she enjoyed making love with Jason because they were not just having sex.)

July 21, 1979: We returned to Atlanta from our honeymoon today. Gilbert would not even look at me at the office. He did call for Jason to come by his office. Jason would not tell me what was said between the two of them in that office.

August 21, 1979: Jason has acted very strange since we returned from our honeymoon. We haven't made love since our honeymoon.

March 5, 1980: We have been married eight months, and Jason is on one of his hunting trips in the mountains. He has been gone for two days now. Gilbert came to the house tonight and came directly to my room. I locked the door and within minutes he was knocking on the door. I wouldn't answer him at all so he kicked down the door. I fought him for a while or as long as I could. Then Gilbert raped me, not once but three times during the night. Gilbert thinks he is so macho, he's sick.

April 24, 1980: I told Jason what had happened and he could have cared less. He cares nothing for me at all. I told Jason to pack it up and move some place else. Now I know Jason was not the man I was looking for to help me fight Skinner.

September 10, 1988: Gilbert told me today that Jason has been stealing money from the company. How much he was stealing he did not know but it would probably reach into the millions. He had been stealing for years. Gilbert told me he could have Jason taken care of, but then he would not get the money. We need to recover that money from him or we will have to answer to the company ourselves.

October 28, 1988: Jason did not commit suicide, if he is dead. I don't believe he is dead.

December 7, 1988: Colby Grey is the investigator that I decided to hire. Mr. Grey has a very professional manner about himself. He also seems to work with loyalty, a man who has pride about his work and about himself. He certainly appears to be an honest man to me.

December 11, 1988: I think I have found the man that I have been looking for my entire life. I am sure Colby is a strong man in every respect. Strong where all other men I've known have been weak. I don't believe anyone could scare him away from any situation. I feel that strongly about this man.

December 16, 1988: I told Gilbert that he would never touch me again. When he started raging and moving toward me, I pulled a .32 pistol from my purse. I told Gilbert I would love to shoot him not only for myself but for my mother too, so don't make it easy for me.

The entry was the night I had dinner with Jennifer and Skinner. She broke it off that night according to her diary. She said the reason she had the strength to stand up to Gilbert at this particular time was because of me. She said she had found the man she wanted and that I was too much of a gentleman to even consider the possibility of the two of us getting together. She added that I might have thought that it was improper to mix business and pleasure. Her last remark about that night was that she was going to have to make the first move.

In the remaining pages, Jennifer wrote of our times together, our one night of love making, how wonderful it

was for her to be treated like a woman, a lady. She had
written about her trip to New York. Jennifer thought she
would be home Christmas Day to spend it with me, but
Gilbert couldn't make it to New York so she had to meet
with the boss. Her having to spend Christmas Day with a
woman was not what she had in mind. All she wanted to do
was be with me and this is what she told the woman she
met with on Christmas Day. She wrote how she had told
her what a special person Colby Grey was to her. She
continued writing about how afraid she was for my life the
night she had gotten back from New York. Gilbert had told
her he was going to kill me if she ever saw me again. Then
she had to fight him off until she pulled her pistol on him
again. He must have cared for her in some form or fashion
because he could have done something about her threats.
She now had something to fight for she said, and it was
Colby Grey. There was no way that she would ever let
Gilbert Skinner touch her again. All the action she wrote
about in Destin was true because I was there on watch.
(Why didn't I take care of Skinner that morning in Destin?
If I had, Jennifer would still be alive?) Skinner had told her
on the flight back to Atlanta that I was a dead man just as
soon as he could find me. Everything in her diary seemed to
fall into place with certain events. Her love for me was the
real thing, a love that made her courageous, noble, and
strong. A supreme love that gives life to the holder. Her last
remark in her diary was a quotation from Byron, "Man's
love is of man's life a part; it is woman's whole existence."

When I finished reading her diary, I knew no one would
ever read the feeling of hurt, her anger, her shame, her
suffering, her disappointments, her torment, and most of all
her wanting revenge so badly. She tried everything to

destroy Skinner. In the end it did destroy her, but I am glad I'm the one who shot the low classed son-of-a-bitch.

I walked over to the fireplace, where I preceded to burn Jennifer's diary, page by page. As it was burning my pain seemed to ease somewhat.

CHAPTER THIRTY-FIVE
SATURDAY, JANUARY 7, 1989

After I had finished with Jennifer's diary it was time to get ready to go to the office. It was 9 A.M. when I finally called John and asked him to meet me at the office. I also made two other calls; one for a taxi and the other call was to Lt. Black asking him to meet us at the office around lunchtime. That would give John and me enough time to listen to the tapes and discuss them. We had missed something in this case, but maybe when we find Traci Love it will all come together. I certainly hope so because I'll feel as if I am letting Jennifer down, even in death. She tried to give me everything I needed to solve this case. It must be solved at all cost whatever it takes. I must find Traci and all the stolen money if indeed it was stolen.

John came in shortly after I arrived. In fact the coffee had not completely finished making. When he entered the office, he was singing. We waited for the coffee to finish so we could enjoy a cup before we settled down to listen and discuss the tapes. After hearing them, we both came to the same conclusions. Either Skinner or Jason is lying; maybe both of them have been lying. Since one of them is dead and one is alive, we have only one starting point. All the evidence left by Jennifer and Skinner pretty much spells out Jason as a thief; and the amount of money that was taken was not known. We had not had time to check Jason out thoroughly. We really don't know how true his statements are. Most of them matched with our findings, but Indian Joe's story was different concerning the fire and killing. Normally, John would have gone to Houston to check everything out after getting Jason to Atlanta. The way everything happened, time had become a factor. That is a piece of sorry detective work on my part. Jennifer, forgive me for letting you down. It won't happen again.

John was going back to Houston to talk with Mark's agency to find out if he had told them anything prior to his death. The Texas Rangers had to be contacted also concerning the evidence gathered by them on the Mark and Martha deaths. He called the airport to book a flight on the first plane departing for Houston, which was scheduled shortly. John actually had less than an hour and a half so he was off and running. Running seems to be part of his regular routine these days. Both of us were getting concerned about Jason. We decided to tell him that John was on his way to Albany, Georgia, to identify a cocaine runner and for him to just hang tight. Jason complained. He wanted to know when he could get out of the apartment. He felt like a caged animal. I could certainly understand where he was coming from, but we had to stall him for at least a couple of more days.

Lt. Black walked in about five minutes before John left for the airport. We explained what we were doing and why. We told him he would understand better after reviewing the tapes. He was with me almost three hours; we ordered lunch and listened to the tapes. This made the third time for me. I could almost repeat them word for word. Lt. Black was thrilled with what he heard. He knew what he heard would solidify the evidence we had on Lt. Day now. There would be no way he could get out of a conviction and prison term of at least 10 years or more.

At 3 P.M., Lt. Black left the office for his precinct. I continued trying to put the pieces together. My thoughts kept returning to Ginny's death. Jennifer had told me she knew nothing of Jason's safe but she was aware of the money being somewhere. Jason's safe was in his office, so she just thought it was there. Jennifer made the statement at one point that she knew Ginny worked for her, but that she had not been told about the money or the list of names. I believe Jennifer, now that it is too late. But this could be an important clue. Jennifer might not have been Ginny's boss after all. Maybe Ginny had been talking about someone else. Traci Love came to my mind. I remember the night Ginny was talking about her boss, she had said 'she' told me to watch out for you, that Colby sounded dangerous.

This afternoon had gone by fast, and the darkness of night crept up without my noticing. When the phone rang, startling me into reality, I couldn't believe time had passed so quickly. I must have been totally focused. Anyway, it was Lt. Black informing me of Rodney Day's arrest and booking. He said, "Colby, thanks to you we have put away another dirty Atlanta cop!" Lt. Black was thrilled. He added, "I made the arrest myself; man did that feel good!" I said, "Great, John Christopher, I'm proud of you."

At 6 P.M., I was completing my work and was on my way to John's apartment to talk with Jason when the phone rang again. It was John calling from Houston. He had not found Mark's remains, and the agency knew nothing about Mark. They had been working on a case outside their agency for about two weeks and did not appear to know anything about Mark's whereabouts. John was at the cabin now searching for Mark's and Martha's bodies. John told me there had been no gun battle there as Jason had reported to us. John did say he found a small trace of blood but nothing that would point to anything big yet. He told me he would keep looking and call me back later.

At 8 P.M., John called again telling me he had found Mark's body buried in a shallow grave behind the cabin. John had been smart enough to take one of Mark's friends from the agency with him to the cabin. Mark had been beaten to death by a blunt instrument. John said that Mark had been dragged to the burial site by two people, that their footprints were still visible and one person's feet were much smaller than the other's was. Most of the footprints had been raked over with some kind of brush. He also related that the Texas Rangers were now on the scene, running around everywhere gathering anything that looked like evidence. John then said that I had better get Lt. Black over to his apartment and hold Jason for questioning. I knew he thought Martha was still alive and that this did not look good for any of us. I wanted to know what he had told the authorities there about our investigation. His comment was, "As little as possible but I may have to divulge more in order to get out of Texas." I told him I would take care of everything in Atlanta but to please call if he needed me.

I told Lt. Black I would meet him at John's apartment in 15 minutes, and I gave him the address. John Christopher knew it would be hard for me to get there, so he was sending a black and white that was already in my area to pick me up. When we got to John's apartment, the officer stationed out front told me that Lt. Black was on his way down and would be here in a matter of minutes. John's relief man who had been staying with Jason had been drugged. Jason had flown the coop. How many mistakes can one private investigator make in one case? I had made enough to last a lifetime.

Lt. Black put an APB on Jason but I didn't have a lot of confidence in the department's APB. Jason was very good at disguising himself to blend in with people. He has had a lot of practice in this area, within the last few months of running and staying undercover. But why did he want to get back to Atlanta? Obviously the money is hidden here some place. Then bells started going off in my head, his townhouse could be where he is now. When Lt. Black and I reached the townhouse, there was a small lamp on, and I knew there was someone there or had been there.

Lt. Black found the townhouse superintendent quickly and told him we needed a pass key to apartment 20. We knocked on the door; there was no answer; we rang the doorbell; there was no answer; at this point we asked the superintendent to unlock the door. The superintendent wanted to protest, but Black quickly reminded him that if we have to wait for a search warrant and miss getting what we need, we would hold him personally responsible. He understood, and the door was unlocked. Lt. Black's power of persuasion is something to see in action.

We walked into the townhouse and knew someone had been there just a short while before. It had to be Jason; it just had to be. He had gotten suspicious about John's trip, or he felt like this was his best time yet to get what he had come to Atlanta for. Lt. Black turned to the superintendent and asked him had he seen anyone in the townhouse complex today other than owners. To our surprise, he related that there was an old man on this same floor about three or four hours ago. I asked him if I could help him with anything, and he said he had already found his friend and was just leaving. Lt. Black called down to one of the cars and told them to get an artist up here fast. We continued to check the townhouse, but there was nothing out of place. Then I noticed something different. The small table at the entrance to the bedroom had recently been moved. I noticed it because of the indentation in the carpet; it was not sitting in the same spot it had been for months. It had been moved just a short while ago. I picked up the table and examined it. There it was! John and I had missed it because the table had a false back. Something of importance had been hidden there. Lt. Black and I examined it very closely avoiding touching anything I had not already touched. There was a small imprint of tape on the back. Someone had done a good job hiding a key. At least that is what it appeared to be to both of us. There is no wonder John and I didn't see it when we were here the first time. By the time we were finished looking and searching, the artist and his computer had finished the drawing of Jason or at least that is who we thought it was anyway. I told Lt. Black I wanted a couple of copies for John and myself. I expected John in by tomorrow, and he will know if this was Jason's disguise.

Finally, we left for John's apartment. I knew, with all the activity that was going on, Jason would not go back to the apartment. When we got back, we stopped and asked the officer stationed outside if he had seen this man and showed him the drawing. He looked at it for a second or two and said, "Yes." After further scrutinizing, he informed us that this person left the premises about an hour after we had departed for the townhouse. The officer looked at me and then looked back at Lt. Black and said, "This fellow has some balls; Sir, he came right up to me and asked what was going on." What we have to do now is outsmart Jason and beat him at his next move.

Lt. Black and I went to the precinct where he could call his complete force in to check all the hotels and motels in Atlanta. I have never been impressed with police handling of missing persons before, but Lt. Black had this hunt well organized in a short time. He had every section of Atlanta walled off and officers in those areas asking questions, showing the drawing to everyone, just out doing their job.

About 20 minutes passed, 1:00 A.M., a female officer called Lt. Black to come to the Atlanta Inn Motel on Highway 85. She reported a possible sighting of the suspect. "In fact, he may be here as we speak," was her comment. We were there within minutes of her call due to little traffic on the streets at this hour of the morning. John Christopher is a good cop; he knows his city.

Jason had rented room 216 on the second floor. The officer in charge went to the room, knocked on the door, but there was no answer. She had gotten a pass key from the night manager and after several attempts to get Jason to the door, she used it. Jason had been there because we found traces of gray hair and someone who likes RC colas. I remember his list of hunting supplies included a case of RC colas.

We figured someone here at the motel had tipped him off. We went back down to speak with the manager. He said there was no way he could have tipped him off because he never left the police officer once she arrived. The officer told Lt. Black that was right, that the two of them had been together the entire time. Then she looked a little pale as if she had seen a ghost. Outside in the parking lot she saw the old man she had questioned earlier about Jason. She immediately went to the old man where he sat drinking his booze. The bottle of bourbon was almost full which wasn't the case the first time she spoke with him. She had shown the old man the drawing and asked him if he had seen this man. This was before she talked with the manager. There were about 10 minutes between the time she had talked with the old man, talking with the manager, and finally calling Lt. Black to report her findings. This had given the old man enough time to warn Jason.

The officer asked the old man where he got his booze, but he didn't respond. When she finally did get his attention, she showed him the drawing again. This time she took another approach to questioning the old man. She asked him if his friend had bought him the booze. The old man smiled and said, "Yes, he gave me fifty bucks." The officer warmly said that he must be a good friend. The old man replied, "Yes he is. All I had to do was look for his son or daughter. He even showed me a picture of his son. They want to put him in the old folks home." Then the old man looked at the officer and Lt. Black and said, "You two should be ashamed of yourselves." The officer said, "Yes sir, I guess we should be but we just want to get Dad to the doctor." "You see," she added, "my Dad is dying and he doesn't even know it." She had tears running down her face. The old man looked closely at her; with tears in his eyes he pointed to the corner and told her he had caught a cab. Lt. Black smiled because he knew his officer had done a beautiful job getting information.

The rest of the night went by without anything happening. We found the cab driver later; he had dropped Jason off in downtown Atlanta close to an all night cafe and a bar across the street. According to the information we received, he had not been seen in either establishment. This is where we lost his trail.

At 3 A.M., Lt. Black took me to my apartment to catch a few hours of sleep. It had been over 24 hours since I had gotten up the morning before. I knew we would find Jason. It would be just a matter of time.

CHAPTER THIRTY-SIX
SUNDAY, JANUARY 8, 1989

The phone woke me at 9 A.M. It was John, who was back in Atlanta. He told me to get out of bed so we could solve this case. John had already talked with Lt. Black about what had occurred last night. He had called me around 2:30 this morning before he left Houston, but I had not gotten back to my apartment until later. He couldn't call again until he got back to Atlanta because his cell phone had gone dead. He then told me he would pick me up in 30 minutes.

When John got there I had showered, shaved and dressed. I had not had enough time to make coffee so we decided to stop by the corner store to pick up a cup. I wanted to know what time he arrived in Atlanta. His reply was that he arrived around 6 A.M. and then he told me what had taken place in Houston the night before. The Texas Rangers did a good, efficient job covering the crime scene. They found a blond hair under one of Mark's fingernails. There was blood on his head that did not match his blood type. The Rangers let me leave because the investigator from Mark's Houston agency was an ex-Ranger, retired with honors and he told them what they wanted to hear. He told them the exact same thing I had told them earlier in the evening. I gave them my cell phone number and your office number and assured them that the office here would know where I was at all times.

We started to talk about Jason, what his plans might be, and why he came to Atlanta. John's reasoning was the same as mine. He came back to Atlanta for the money. Since today is Sunday, he will have a problem getting to a safe deposit box or should I say several safe deposit boxes. Safe deposit boxes may not have been his chosen mode of securing the stolen money. He could have used lockers - all over town; at the airport, train depot, sport complexes or gyms, and even the bus station. Lt. Black already had his officers out about the city checking people and places and with them were two artist renditions of Jason, one as himself and one in the disguise he wore back from Houston. Lt. Black then added that he feels like we have everything covered for the time being.

John believes that Martha is still alive and somewhere in Atlanta. We usually think about the same way when it comes to clues concerning the case. Jason could have given her a key during the night. We also knew they could be wearing disguises whenever they might appear. They have become pros at what they are doing; they may be together or they may be traveling alone. That means everyone going to a box or locker has to be checked out real carefully. We both feel that together they killed Mark. I had caught Jason in several lies about one thing or another, but I guess my mind was preoccupied too much with Jennifer to see what was going on right under my nose. Then think about the money. Millions of dollars will make a person do things they never dreamed of doing before.

Lt. Black had all the areas covered by the time John had picked me up this morning. He must have at least a hundred extra officers working different spots in Atlanta. Keeping everything under wraps is what Lt. Black is good at. He is an organizer and believe you me, he is doing an excellent job with this case. John Christopher knew how to situate his officers in order to get maximum coverage. He is truly one of Atlanta's finest.

John and I must have gone over everything that has
happened in the case at least twice before lunch. There was
not a clue as to who Traci Love is or where she could be
found. Then something hit me directly in the face. After
checking with the telephone company, I found out where a
certain phone call came from. It confirmed my thoughts, I
was right. I should have thought about this sooner. Why
would she make a statement like that to me? I called Lt.
Black to tell him of my plan. He was just as surprised as I
was when it hit me moments ago. He told me he would
keep tabs on everything in Atlanta. Then I told him I
wanted an officer on loan for the rest of the case. John said
he was sure he could find me a good man. At that I said,
"Well, John, I would love to have the female officer who
handled the situation with the old man last evening." He
agreed that was a good choice.

When Officer Ami Adams got to my office, John and I
enlightened her about everything. We told her where we
were going and explained that she will travel there also but
she would be trailing Jason or Martha. We told Ami this
was not the exact scenario, but we believed things would
happen in this way. We cautioned her to be careful because
these two had already killed, and they would do it again.
We instructed her to give them plenty of distance and not to
take chances but protect herself at all times. Then I wanted
to know if she had any problem with being on loan to us. If
she didn't, I would expect her to be as loyal to me as she is
to Lt. Black. She let me know in a hurry that she had no
problem at all. John told her that it was a good paying job,
and she laughed out loud.

Now that we have all investigative matters in order, John
and I are off to get ourselves personally ready for our trip.

The first stop I made was the hospital. I wanted to get this cast off and have a smaller one put on. The doctor had no problem with removing the leg cast and putting on a walking cast. Incidentally, the cast he replaced it with was a boot cast made for walking. It felt like a heavy boot on my foot, but it did the job for my leg.

When we caught our flight out of Atlanta, we had our disguises on. I had a gray beard, wore a gray business suit, and my mannerisms were very businesslike. John was dressed as a man of the sea, whatever that means. He did appear to be an experienced sea captain on his way to his next assignment. We were not flying together, but our desires to solve this case were in unison. We flew out of Atlanta at 3:15 P.M. and if everything goes as we have planned, this case will be solved tomorrow. If it doesn't go as we have planned, Lt. Black will be able to reach us in a hurry so we can change our strategy to the situation we encounter.

Now that I can walk everything will be much easier for me. I feel like I'm almost a whole man again; I can walk and move around like I once did.

CHAPTER THIRTY-SEVEN
SUNDAY, JANUARY 8, 1989

We landed at John F. Kennedy airport in New York at 4:58 P.M. and this gave us plenty of time to get things rolling. We had to go by the terminal's main office to retrieve our weapons and while we were there we spoke with the CEO of the airport, Kyle Henderson. We needed to use the viewing room tonight and tomorrow in order to check out the comings and goings of passengers. We emphasized the importance of his cooperation and to validate our request we gave him Lt. Black's number in Atlanta. After a lengthy conversation with Lt. Black, everything was finally legalized by documents that were received via fax.

In the viewing room, we could see every passenger getting on and off every flight. It was amazing. Kyle provided us with schedules of every flight arriving from Atlanta. We were able to narrow down the flights which left Atlanta that flew to another city and then finally arrived in New York. There were flights to Memphis, New Orleans, St. Louis, Cincinnati and Washington. There were also two flights coming straight from Atlanta to New York.

We had to be ready for anything tonight, tomorrow, or whenever it happened. We had to be ready! Hunger reared its head, so we ordered lunch and ate as we carried out our tedious task. Watching incoming planes unload is not as easy as it sounds. Thank God for this viewing room. It is great. If we spot them we can cut them off before they get out of the terminal if we need to. We want to get everyone involved if at all possible. We want to get the money also.

We may have to tail them, but hopefully, this won't be necessary.

The night was a long one because there were only two flights coming in from Atlanta. We got no help from Atlanta, but we didn't' really expect anything before tomorrow anyway. About 8 A.M. John said, "Look at the flight from Houston. The red head is Martha Rogers." John was right; the woman was Martha Rogers, and she was here for their rendezvous before leaving the country we assumed. I told John to tail her but to keep in touch. They had given us a straight phone line to the viewing room in case this occurred, as we needed constant contact with each other. Emergencies can occur. I continued to check people coming in from Atlanta and different places, but there was nothing I saw that I felt would help us.

John had been gone for about an hour, maybe an hour and a half, when he called. Martha had picked up one piece of luggage on her way out of the airport. He then tailed Martha downtown New York to the Empire Hotel. John was impressed with the Empire Hotel. "It is a real classic." he said. John had overheard Martha ask the desk clerk for Trawynette Lovstrom's room. The desk clerk replied that this would have to be cleared with Ms. Lovstrom. He called the room and informed the occupant that she had a visitor. At this point the clerk turned and asked Martha her name and strangely she said her name was Marlene Gentry. There was another pause in the conversation while he listened to the clerk. He then told Martha that Ms. Lovstrom's room number was 626 on the sixth floor and that Ms. Lovstrom was waiting. John then said that he was going to sit tight to see what happened. He told me he would let me know when something else happened.

Here I am in New York waiting for a needle in a haystack to appear. I only hope my calculations are right; if they are then we will solve Jason Myland's case. The solution could be dated January 9, 1989. To tell you the truth, this has been one of the most mixed up cases I have been involved with since becoming a private investigator. One reason it has been so mixed up is because I had my mind so screwed up. There were too many things on my mind other than the case. Even though Jennifer lost her life, she got revenge on Gilbert Skinner for what he had done to her mother and her. I wonder if I will ever be able to completely get over this case or Jennifer. Love is like money in many ways because the human race will do most anything to have either one of them.

Lt. Black had been given this number when he was called to verify John and myself. I knew if anything had happened he would have called. Time was moving and nothing was happening at the airport. John had not called back so I'm assuming everything was the same at the Empire. Thoughts kept running through my mind, and I kept asking myself how Martha and Traci knew each other. They must have met through Jason. But if Traci was the big boss, why would Jason have stolen cocaine money? Good question and why were Ginny and Mark killed? There was no reason for their deaths; those were senseless murders. These unnecessary murders had no rhyme or reason.

The phone rang and startled me. Maybe something is about to happen! It was Lt. Black telling me Ami was loading Delta flight number 424 to New York as we spoke. I knew she had found Jason and was tailing him to New York. I had plenty of time to relive many of the events that had occurred during the case while waiting for flight 424 to arrive. I knew Jennifer didn't lie to herself in her diary. A diary is being honest to one's self because it is so personal and very private. Jennifer had put too many honest and personal comments in her diary not to tell the entire truth. There were comments about certain things that would be only important to her. I was too involved with my own hurt to grab hold of the clues in front of me. There were those honest statements made to herself in her own private world that made my mind begin to function again. I started to remember certain things that had happened during the past month that enabled me to begin to solve the case, to fit parts and mysteries together that lead to a conclusion. The puzzle pieces began to fit in their proper places and the entire picture became visible, thanks to Jennifer's diary.

There are several things that still bother me, but maybe I can work these out after today. The phone interrupted my thoughts. It was Lt. Black asking if the flight from Atlanta had arrived. I told him it should be here within the hour, and I would be in touch with him as soon as possible. I hung up the phone, but only for a few seconds because it rang again. It was John. He told me he was in a cab following two very lovely older women. He continued telling me the story during the cab ride. He had overheard

the desk clerk tell a bell hop to go to room 626 to pick up
Ms. Lovstrom's luggage. He stated that Ms. Lovstrom was
checking out. John decided he had better get himself a cab
on hold so he could be dead set on ready when they
departed. John also said this would enable him to follow at
a safe distance rather than chase from afar. I finally
interrupted him with the information that Jason was on his
way to New York. We had their rendezvous pegged right
for sure! Jason should be here within the hour and their
little plans will be interrupted, if all goes well. Why was
Martha in the picture? We thought Jason had killed her
after the two of them killed Mark in Houston. The body
was never found, true, so it was not really a surprise when I
learned she was alive. John pointed out that Martha was
very much alive and very attractive in her disguise. When
he started to tell me how Ms. Lovstrom looked, I stopped
him, pausing a few seconds before telling him how her
disguise looked without even having seen it. He laughed
and said, "HOW RIGHT YOU ARE COLBY." He then
told me they had turned and were traveling toward the
airport. "Stay close," were my last words as we hung up.

At that moment, we had word from air traffic control that
flight 424 from Atlanta was on schedule and was now
approaching the terminal and would be landing in about 15
minutes. The time is perfect for the rendezvous, if this is
indeed "The Rendezvous"! The phone rang again; it was
John relaying the latest. The two women had stopped at a
used car lot just outside the airport area. They must have
purchased a car earlier because they have loaded their
luggage into the vehicle. Ms. Lovstrom is driving and they
are approaching the parking area now. I told John to stay

with them, that I had to go because the flight from Atlanta was landing. "Stay with the car," I shouted as I hung up the phone.

Our plan was for me to meet Ami as she disembarked the plane. I was disguised as her father, and was in a wheelchair with a blanket over my lap and legs. The blanket was used to hide the cast on my foot. The attendant that was pushing me was an airport security person and had been instructed to assist if something went wrong. Of course, the plan began on the flight. One of the flight attendants had been filled in before they left Atlanta and had agreed to help. During the flight, she moved Ami to a seat in front of Jason, explaining that Ami was to help her sick father at the airport. She also explained that she needed to be the first passenger to exit as this was an emergency situation. This move did not seem to trigger any element of suspicion with Jason.

Ami disembarked first and ran straight to me. Jason was three people behind us as we all moved toward the baggage claim area. Jason was disguised as an old man; but to be honest, he moved as if he was a much younger man. Not very believable, right? Anyway he soon caught and passed us. At this point, Ami increased our speed in order to keep up with Jason. Ami briefed me as to how she spotted Jason at the airport. She had returned to the motel to speak with Jason's informant, the old man who was in the parking lot. She found him and by playing on his sympathy, was able once again to obtain information. She again spoke of Jason as her own father, how he was a well-liked and loved gentleman. During their conversation Ami asked the old man what stood out about her father to him and surprisingly he said, "the hat, I love that ole brown Stetson with the plaid band." Bingo! It was time to go. Ami gave the old man a ten spot and told him to get himself a warm meal.

We continued moving as Jason got further away from us, but our security guard stayed as close to him as possible. We got to the baggage claim area in time to see Martha meet Jason. They embraced with a long kiss as Martha passed a paper bag to him. He inconspicuously slipped it into his inner coat pocket. My conclusion is that the bag contained a weapon.

Jason grabbed two pieces of luggage and they headed toward the exit. Ami had already retrieved her small piece of luggage, and we were now only a few steps behind Jason. All of a sudden a woman began yelling at the top of her voice, "They have stolen my bag!" "The man in the wheelchair has my bag," she continued. This distracted Martha and Jason enough to cause them to turn back and take a good look at the situation in action. They continued to move hurriedly, but the yell had alerted security and by this time we were surrounded as our two suspects slipped away. They began questioning us. Finally our security guard stepped in and informed security that we were okay. The yelling woman suddenly began to yell again, "It's okay, I found my bag! I found my bag! Their bag is almost identical to mine," she explained at the top of her voice. I thought to myself, "How stupid can some people be,

KNOW what you are talking about before you make a scene."

We were on our way again but we had lost some valuable time. As we reached the front, we saw Jason and Martha reach their car. They were putting the luggage in the trunk as we finally began to free ourselves from the crowd the yelling woman had gathered. Ami was pushing the chair as fast as she could. John saw what was happening with us and he shouted, "That's far enough Jason, put your hands on your head and move away from the car." All of a sudden, a gunshot went off and John fell to the ground. John was apparently hit. Ami left me; she was running toward Jason and Martha and a flash from a pistol coming from the area of the car went off. Then I saw Ami take aim and fire twice at Martha. Martha went down, falling backward against Jason and the car. Martha had been the one doing the shooting because Jason was just getting his pistol out of the paper bag. He was able to get off a couple of shots at Ami before I had a clear shot at him. One of his shots hit Ami because out of the corner of my eye I saw her fall. I fired Sara twice hitting Jason both times sending him hard against the car. There was one more shot fired by Jason but it must have been when he hit the car because by the time I got to him he was dead. Martha was dead also. Ms. Lovstrom, the driver of the car, had been wounded. She had been hit in the chest, but she was still alive - barely. By this time we had security guards and New York police everywhere trying to figure out what had happened. The security guard that had been assigned to us was explaining everything to them.

I got to Ami as quickly as I could because she was closer to me than John was. She was moving around telling me to check on John because she was only scratched and was okay. I finally found John; he was not moving. "Oh my God, John was dead," I thought. I began calling for medical assistance. When the paramedics examined John, it was determined that he had only been hit in the shoulder but when he fell he had received a head injury from hitting his head on the curb. He was only knocked out, causing him to miss all the excitement. This will really make John mad because once he starts something he wants to be in on all the action. Well, John has missed the final climax of this case.

The emergency team prior to transporting them to the hospital patched up John and Ami. Both of them grossly objected, but their complaint was ignored because the law says a physician must see them before being released. Thank God for that. Two officers accompanied Ms. Lovstrom to the hospital while Ami and John were transported separately.

As soon as I completed my paperwork and reported to Lt. Black, I was on my way to the hospital to pick up two fine assistants and to find out the condition of Ms. Lovstrom. After the release of Ami and John, we immediately went to check on her. She was being prepared for surgery and the physician advised that she had less than a 50/50 percent chance of surviving the procedure. She sustained a gunshot wound from close range. It must have caused a lot of damage and was apparently from the last shot Jason fired. The assisting surgeon explained that if she did make it through surgery, she still only had a slim chance for survival.

While waiting for the news of Ms. Lovstrom's operation, I told John what a real trooper Ami had been. She had performed wonderfully in the face of the enemy, especially during those very dangerous moments. Ami was beginning to blush a little so I stopped my comments about her. Then I told both of them what a great job they had done and that I personally appreciated it, and the agency appreciated it also. John said, "Thanks Colby, just show us HOW much in 'green stuff'." Of course, he was ribbing me, releasing some of the tension we had all been under for the past few days. I just had to continue the lighthearted mood and replied, "No problem, you'll receive your normal $1 per hour." We all laughed. Then I asked Ami how she liked detective work now that she had a taste of the action. Her response was very positive; she said she really enjoyed it. She liked being part of the team. Well, needless to say, I was very impressed with her performance this afternoon.

At the time the Chief of New York's finest arrived and reported they had confiscated over $10,000,000 in the five pieces of luggage they found in the trunk of the car. That meant Jason had been shaving a great deal off the top of Skinner's dirty cocaine money. No wonder Skinner was having a fit about Jason. Jason was destroying the entire operation.

The doctor interrupted our thoughts and conversation by telling us we could see Ms. Lovstrom for a minute. She has been out of surgery and recovery for a few hours. The doctor still had no hope for her making it through the night, although, there had been miracles before in cases such as this. My thought was that maybe she would be one tonight. He continued telling us she was awake enough to talk a little. I only wanted some answers. My big concern was if she could talk, would she be honest with me? Maybe she would be completely honest because she knows that I have put most of the case together by now. I asked the doctor if she knew she might die and he replied, "Yes, Mr. Grey, she does."

As we entered the room, I could see her lying there with a look of defeat on her face. The pain she was enduring was minimal because of the drugs they were administering to her. I walked over to the bed and said, "Hello, Joan, or should I call you Joyce or maybe Traci." She looked at me with eyes that were very cold and full of hatred. That lasted for only a moment when her facial expression changed, and she softly spoke to me. She was barely audible but by leaning over and placing my ear close to her mouth I heard her say, "I will tell all if you will only take care of my son." I promised I would. When she finished telling me her story, she could hardly talk above a whisper. Her nurse stepped in and said that Joan was very exhausted and needed her rest. We left with many answers, thanks to her brief story.

Upon returning to the waiting room, John and Ami expressed their desire to hear what Traci had told me. Of

course, they were anxious. I was as nervous as a cat prior
to talking with Traci. Anyway, they patiently sat there
spellbound as I related the story. Ms. Lovstrom or Traci and
Martha were half-sisters, with the same mother and
different fathers. I related that they were very close as
children and had remained so throughout their lives. Traci
was the older of the two by three years and her real name
was Trawynette Lovstrom. Martha's birth name was
Marlene Gentry. Traci's father owned the tobacco
company. He was an old man when he passed away, but
Martha's father was only forty when he was killed in an
automobile accident. Martha was two years old when this
occurred. Raising two girls must have been difficult. Their
mother had struggled as a single parent for a few years
when she met this man who had just graduated from college
and was hired by the tobacco company. She fell madly in
love with him, and they were married a year later. His name
was Gilbert Skinner and their marriage turned out to be a
very bitter one. Gilbert wanted control of the company.
Their mother had been very smart; she had given the
company to her girls prior to the wedding. The gift and the
stipulations of it were so ironclad that no one could operate
the company other than the girls, even their mother could
never have any say-so after the agreement was legalized.
Finally, this became too much for Gilbert; and he left
Boston. Their mother blamed herself and literally grieved
herself to death.

After her death, Gilbert was free, so that is when he went
after Jennifer's mother. Their engagement announcement
made the national news. When you're one of the wealthiest
women in the United States, all eyes are on your every

move. So Traci saw the announcement, and she now knew Gilbert's location. A trip to Atlanta was imminent.

Eventually Traci went to Atlanta, landed a job interview at the Building of Glass, and met Jason. Jason was so taken with her that he hired her after the first interview. Traci and Martha had set their plan into action. The ultimate goal was to destroy Gilbert Skinner, the object of their hatred. Very little Joan (or Traci or Joyce) told me was true. She did say she and Jason were lovers before and after his marriage to Jennifer. The marriage was part of their plan to destroy Gilbert Skinner. Then Gilbert put a hit man on Jason, and of course, he had to run for his life. He went into hiding in Houston. Martha carried money to Houston every time she went to her so called home. Jason wanted the movement of the money to be a slow easy process so they could retrieve all of it unnoticed. Then Jennifer hired me and within a few days we had put the fear of God in Martha, and she went directly to Jason in Houston. They thought John was one of Skinner's hit men and that is why they were running when we caught them in Mexico. The reason Joan came to Atlanta was to throw me off Jason's trail long enough to allow them to retrieve the remaining money. I didn't tell John and Ami this, but at the end of the conversation, she told me Jennifer was a lucky woman to have me to love and in return for me to have loved her so much.

John's only question was what about Traci's son? Was Jason the father? I related that Traci said she had met Anthony, a football player, while in college. They fell in love, were married, and had a wonderful son.

Unfortunately, her husband was killed three months after their marriage and never really knew for sure if Traci was pregnant. At the time of his death, Anthony was taking private flying lessons when the plane caught fire. He and the instructor were unable to parachute out of the plane before it exploded in mid-air.

John and Ami went out to dinner, and I asked them to bring me a carry-out so I would be near Traci in case she wanted to see me again. I'm glad I did because a nurse came to me just 15 minutes later and said Traci was asking for me and that I didn't have much time. Upon arriving at her side, I whispered that I was there and asked what could I do for her. She told me the name of her attorney in Boston. He had all her records, will and assets, to take care of her son's interests. She wanted to be sure that I would take care of him. She had made copies of everything the attorney had in his possession, and these copies were filed in her office. She wanted me to write down exactly what she wanted done. At this point, the nurse produced paper and a pen, and I began to write. She must have told the nurse what she was about to do because she had the paper before her request was spoken to me. The nurse had gotten two other nurses as witnesses; one was the head nurse and she was a notary. Traci gave me the power of attorney for her son, Anthony. She wanted me to make sure he received all she had left him. She also wanted me to make sure he was never mistreated by anyone. I wrote down everything she said including the combination to her office safe. When I finished, she scribbled her name on the bottom of the paper and the head nurse took care of the rest of the business. She notarized the papers and put them in an envelope. She also stated that I was welcome to keep the papers in the hospital safe until my return to Atlanta. I kindly refused this offer. I wanted that paper on my being at all times. I did request a letter from her stating what had occurred and that these were Traci's last wishes, just in case Traci didn't make it. I also asked the other two nurses to sign the letter as witnesses.

When I started to leave, Traci said, "Colby, make sure Anthony is put in a good home with a good family." I promised her again that I would take care of Anthony's every need. She looked at me with eyes that said, "Thank you Colby." They were weak eyes, but they still had the class that I saw in them the first time we met. She wanted me to come closer. When I reached her side she wanted me to come even closer and as I leaned down she kissed me on the ear and said, "Thanks Colby Grey." She closed her eyes and drifted off into a deep sleep. The deepest of all sleeps came within minutes after she gave me the kiss.

When John and Ami returned with my food, I was no longer hungry. Even though I was not hungry, I knew I must eat something while telling them what had just happened. I was so exhausted and ready to fly back to Atlanta. This case has been solved, come what may.

EPILOGUE

All the answers I needed were right in front of me. It only took Jennifer's diary to wake me up to the facts. After reading her diary, I knew Joan had not been truthful about the things she volunteered to me. Jennifer and Ginny were not lovers; there was no way they were gay or homosexual. I knew this, but she had planted the thought in my mind to make me wonder about Jennifer. If they had been lovers, it would have consumed a major part of Jennifer's diary. Also, Joan had said a couple of things that made me wonder about her honesty. For instance, during the time I was so worried about the safety of her and her family during their stay in New Orleans, Joan reported that there was no phone service at the motel. Then she slipped by telling me she could see why Jennifer thought I was so special. Jennifer had not seen her since she hired me for the case unless it was in New York. If it was in New York, Joan had to be Traci Love.

Ginny had told me her boss (indicating her boss was a female) had told her to be careful of this man (meaning me), and I thought it was Jennifer who had said it until I read Jennifer's diary. That meant Skinner had ordered Ginny's death.

Jennifer had written in her diary that her meeting before Christmas was canceled because the representative was out of town. That meeting was with a female and it was rescheduled for Christmas Day. The representative was the very same person Jennifer had told (on Christmas Day) how special her Colby was to her.

Jason came back to Atlanta to get the remaining money that Martha had not been able to get to Houston. When John went back to Houston, this was the perfect time for Jason to make his move and he did. Then there was the mystery of Martha's body. According to Jason, Martha had been killed during the shoot out in Houston; but not one time did Jason ask about her. The funeral, the body, or was she in fact dead was of no interest to him. He knew where she was and when he would see her again if indeed he had not killed her.

The fact that Jason would not talk about Joan was another thing that made me wonder. In fact he was always short and to the point when a conversation concerning Joan took place. It appeared as if he was afraid he would let something slip, in retrospect. Finally and most importantly, there were the lies Jason and Martha told about the cabin fire and the death of her husband. Indian Joe had told me the truth about what had happened at Kennesaw Mountain.

Everything pointed to Joan being Traci Love but we had to have positive proof. We figured Joan and Jason were in love. We thought Jason had killed Martha in Houston, but I explained why we changed our minds on this matter.

The amount of money the New York Police Department found in Traci's car was the positive proof we needed.

It has been six months since we closed the Jason Myland case. With all the information in Traci's safe, I was able to do what she wanted me to do with Anthony. He has a wonderful family and Jean and Cory Young let me have him every weekend. Also they have given him that family that Traci wanted so desperately for him to have.

Anthony has his own tobacco company selling only tobacco in Boston. He also has a couple of huge bank accounts abroad. At 21 he will be one of the wealthiest men in America.

Ami and John work well together. After the New York incident she decided that being a private investigator was more exciting than being one of Atlanta's finest. I am very happy to have her as part of my team.

The money Jennifer left me was put to good use. The four of us took $50,000 each and put the rest into a fund for the agency for the future. You never know when the agency may need a little help, COME WHAT MAY.